Managing Editor
Mara Ellen Guckian

Editor in Chief
Karen J. Goldfluss, M.S. Ed.

Creative Director
Sarah M. Smith

Cover Artist
Barb Lorseyedi

Art Coordinator
Renée Mc Elwee

Illustrator
Clint McKnight

Imaging
James Edward Grace
Amanda R. Harter

Publisher
Mary D. Smith, M.S. Ed.

Author
Tracie Heskett, M.Ed.

For correlations to the Common Core State Standards, see page 7.
Correlations can also be found at *http://www.teachercreated.com/standards*

Teacher Created Resources
6421 Industry Way
Westminster, CA 92683
www.teachercreated.com

ISBN: 978-1-4206-3990-2

Made in U.S.A.

Table of Contents

Introduction 3
How to Use This Book 3
Internet Resources 5
National Health Education Standards 6
Common Core State Standards 7
Take the Pledge 8
What Makes a Healthy Food? 9
Healthy Foods Come in Groups 10
Exercise for a Healthier Life 11

Healthy Foods

Fruits

Think About Fruit 13
Growing Fruit 15
Stone Fruits 16
How Well Do You Know Melons? 17
Dragon Fruit 18
Bunches of Bananas 19

Vegetables

Think About Vegetables 20
Different Kinds of Vegetables 22
Culinary Vegetables Crossword 23
Peppers 25
Vegetable Family Tree 27
All Kinds of Squash 28
Leafy Greens and Dark Green Vegetables 30
Growing Vegetables in Small Places 31

Grains

Think About Grains 32
Corn 33
Whole Grains 34
What Does Gluten-Free Mean? 35
Whole Grains—Spotlight on Sorghum 36

Dairy

Think About Dairy Foods 37
Types of Milk 38
Not All Milk Comes from Cows 39
Say Cheese! 40
Fun with Dairy Facts 41

Protein

Think About Protein Foods 42
Types of Protein 43
Do You Know Your Food Animals? 44
All Kinds of Nuts 45
Wild About Seeds 46
Fish and Shellfish Crossword 47
Legumes 49

Making Healthy Food Choices

Local Foods 50
Organic Foods 51
What's in Your Food? 52
Look at the Label! 53
What Counts as One Serving? 54
Calories 56
Natural Sugar and Added Sugar 57
What Is Fiber? 59
What Is Cholesterol? 60
Sodium in Foods 61
Add More Fruits and Vegetables! 62
My Plate—Revised! 63
Food Tips for Tip-Top Health 64

Healthy Habits

Food Safety 65
Sleep Is Good for Us 66
Protect Your Lungs 67
Pathway to Health 68
Stranger Danger 69
Healthy Lifestyles 70
Staying Fit 71
Interval Training 72
You Are a Fitness Machine! 73
Fitness Survey 74
Case for Fitness 75
Sports 76
Think Like an Athlete 77
Careers in the Health Industry 78
Healthy Habits Review 79
Food and Fitness Journal 80
Answer Key 92

Introduction

The *Healthy Habits for Healthy Kids* series was created to provide educators and parents with simple activities that help students learn to make healthy food choices, appreciate the importance of daily exercise, and develop healthy habits they will maintain throughout their lifetimes. Students who are healthy are better able to learn and be successful.

The activities in this book help students understand where the foods they eat come from and why nutritious food choices are beneficial to them. The objectives outlined by the USDA Food Guidance System *(ChooseMyPlate.gov)* formed the foundation upon which the activities in this book are based. Each of the five food groups is explored in depth. The goal is to build an understanding of the need to incorporate fruits, vegetables, whole grains, protein, and dairy into our daily diet. Students will also explore "sometimes" foods, or treats, and develop a greater understanding of why enjoying those foods in moderation is important to his or her health.

Physical fitness is also of the utmost importance for growing children, and it is suggested that they get at least 60 minutes per day of moderate to vigorous activity. At school and at home this can be difficult, since there is always so much to do. Still, knowing how important physical fitness is, we have to try! We have provided a variety of effective suggestions for exercises that can be done in the classroom. They can be completed in short increments on a daily basis. In addition to the obvious benefits of physical activity, the inclusion of purposeful physical activity at strategic times of the day can release tension and energize both students and teacher.

In recent years, the Common Core State Standards have been developed and are being implemented in many schools. These standards aim to prepare students for college and careers, with an emphasis on real-life applications. Coupled with the National Health Education Standards, they support a whole-child approach to education—one that ensures that each student is healthy, safe, engaged, supported, and challenged in his or her learning. The *Healthy Habits for Healthy Kids* series was developed to support this initiative.

How to Use This Book

The *Healthy Habits for Healthy Kids* series was developed to provide busy teachers and students with an easy-to-use curriculum to learn more about personal nutrition, health, and fitness. We want students to embrace making healthy food choices and getting exercise every day, knowing that healthier students make better learners.

Getting Started

- Share the Healthy Habits Pledge (page 8) with students and discuss each line. Challenge students to learn the pledge and share it with family members. The goal here is to inspire the whole family to focus on good nutrition and support healthy habits.
- Post the pledge in the classroom and review it from time to time as students gain more insights into their personal health.
- Introduce daily exercise and breathing activities in class. On pages 11–12 you will find suggestions for breathing exercises and movements that students can do for a minute or two at different times during the day. Display a clock with a second hand or keep a timer handy for these sessions. Use the physical activities to start the day and/or to transition from one activity to another. Throw in an extra session on tough days, or use more than one when weather conditions inhibit outdoor activity. These short, physical exercise breaks are a positive way to settle students for their day's work. And don't forget those breathing exercises! They can be done at any time of day and can help refocus or calm students as needed.

Introduction *(cont.)*

How to Use This Book *(cont.)*

Getting Started *(cont.)*

- Gather and display reference materials for the classroom on topics of nutrition, fitness, and overall health. Resources might include library or trade books, magazines, posters, and kid-friendly materials printed from government websites (see page 5). If appropriate, save links to relevant websites in a dedicated folder on classroom computers.
- Encourage students to start collecting packaging and nutritional labels from food products. Explain that they will be learning to read them and using them for comparisons. Establish an area in the classroom where these can be stored or displayed.

The Student Pages

Student pages present health-related information and activities. Discuss the information together as a class. Share information. Most activities require no more than writing implements and classroom research materials. Devote a certain amount of time each day or week to these activities. The more regular they are, the more important they will be for students.

You might consider interspersing the Healthy Foods activities with Healthy Habits activities to give students a balanced approach. As the teacher, you know how much information your students can absorb at a time. It is also important to be sensitive to the dietary needs and family eating habits of your students.

There are three sections to this book. The first section, Healthy Foods, focuses on the five food groups as described in government materials such as *ChooseMyPlate.gov*. The goal here is to educate students about healthy foods—what they look like, where they come from, what nutrients they provide, and how they can be incorporated into one's diet. A list of the foods in the food group is found at the beginning of each section. Have students think about the foods they eat regularly, the foods they have not heard of before, and healthy foods they would like to try. Provide resource materials for students to learn about foods that are new to them. Encourage students to think about ways they can make healthy food choices each day. Students will also learn about nutrition, including calories, carbohydrates, protein, vitamins, and minerals, and the roles these nutrients play in overall health.

In the Healthy Habits section, students are introduced to concepts such as food safety, germ prevention, dental care, physical fitness, and other ways to stay safe and healthy.

Fruits
Grains
Dairy
Vegetables
Protein
ChooseMyPlate.gov

The final section of this book is devoted to journaling. The Food and Fitness Journal gives students the opportunity to express their thoughts about the information presented in the activities and class discussions. It can be used for reflective writing, sorting or summarizing information, or to check for understanding.

Reproduce copies of the journal pages (pages 80–91) for each student. You may wish to have students add pages to the journal throughout the year as new food and fitness topics arise. Students can add notebook paper to their journals, or you can reproduce extra copies of the blank journal page provided on page 91.

The CD includes ready-to-print PDF files of the student activity pages and the Food and Fitness Journal, as well as correlations to the Common Core State Standards and the National Health Education Standards.

Internet Resources

These sites provide useful, age-appropriate information to aid you in embarking on a year filled with active, healthy students. Let's move!

Action for Healthy Kids
This site provides information for schools, students, and parents, as well as programs to promote active, healthy lifestyles for kids.
http://www.actionforhealthykids.org/

CDC BAM! Body and Mind
This site was designed for 9–13-year-olds. BAM! provides information kids need to make healthy lifestyle choices.
http://www.cdc.gov/bam/teachers/index.html

Fresh for Kids
This site offers resources for kids and teachers, including informative pages on specific fruits and vegetables.
http://www.freshforkids.com.au

Let's Move! America's Move to Raise a Healthier Generation of Kids
This program was developed by First Lady Michelle Obama to solve the epidemic of childhood obesity.
http://www.letsmove.gov/

National Farm to School Network
This site offers resources and information about farm-to-school programs in each state.
http://www.farmtoschool.org/

Nourish Interactive
This site offers free printable activities based on the *ChooseMyPlate.gov* food groups.
http://www.nourishinteractive.com/nutrition-education

Tips for Healthy Eating—Ten Healthy Habits for Kids
This site includes a summary of ways families can incorporate healthy eating habits.
http://www.nestle.com/nhw/health-wellness-tips/healthy-habits-kids

USDA—United States Department of Agriculture
This site includes kid-friendly research, printable materials, and Nutrition Fact Cards.
http://www.choosemyplate.gov/print-materials-ordering.html

The Whole Child
This site focuses on ensuring that each child, in each school and in each community is healthy, safe, engaged, supported, and challenged to meet the demands of the 21st century.
http://www.wholechildeducation.org/

Whole Grains Council
The Whole Grains Council wants to support everyone who's helping spread the word about the health benefits of whole grains, and about easy ways to find and enjoy more whole grains.
http://wholegrainscouncil.org/resources/educational-materials

National Health Education Standards

The activities in *Healthy Habits for Healthy Kids* (Grades 5 and up) meet the following National Health Education Standards. For more information about these standards, go to *www.cdc.gov/healthyyouth/sher/standards/index.htm*

Standard 1.	**Students will comprehend concepts related to health promotion and disease prevention to enhance health.**
Standard 1.5.1	Describe the relationship between healthy behaviors and personal health.
Standard 1.8.1	Analyze the relationship between healthy behaviors and personal health.
Standard 1.5.3	Describe ways in which safe and healthy school and community environments can promote personal health.
Standard 1.8.3	Analyze how the environment affects personal health.
Standard 1.8.4	Describe how family history can affect personal health.
Standard 1.5.4	Describe ways to prevent common childhood injuries and health problems.
Standard 1.8.5	Describe ways to reduce or prevent injuries and other adolescent health problems.
Standard 1.5.5	Describe when it is important to seek health care.
Standard 1.8.6	Explain how appropriate health care can promote personal health.
Standard 1.8.7	Describe the benefits of and barriers to practicing healthy behaviors.
Standard 1.8.8	Examine the likelihood of injury or illness if engaging in unhealthy behaviors.
Standard 2.	**Students will analyze the influence of family, peers, culture, media, technology, and other factors on health behaviors.**
Standard 2.5.1	Describe how family influences personal health practices and behaviors.
Standard 2.5.2	Identify the influence of culture on health practices and behaviors.
Standard 2.5.3	Identify how peers can influence healthy and unhealthy behaviors.
Standard 2.5.4	Describe how the school and community can support personal health practices and behaviors.
Standard 2.5.5	Explain how media influences thoughts, feelings, and health behaviors.
Standard 2.5.6	Describe ways that technology can influence personal health.
Standard 3.	**Students will demonstrate the ability to access valid information, products, and services to enhance health.**
Standard 3.5.1	Identify characteristics of valid health information, products, and services.
Standard 3.5.2	Locate resources from home, school, and community that provide valid health information.
Standard 3.8.1	Analyze the validity of health information, products, and services.
Standard 4.	**Students will demonstrate the ability to use interpersonal communication skills to enhance health and avoid or reduce health risks.**
Standard 4.5.1	Demonstrate effective verbal and nonverbal communication skills to enhance health.
Standard 4.5.2	Demonstrate refusal skills that avoid or reduce health risks.
Standard 5.	**Students will demonstrate the ability to use decision-making skills to enhance health.**
Standard 5.5.1	Identify health-related situations that might require a thoughtful decision.
Standard 5.5.3	List healthy options to health-related issues or problems.
Standard 5.5.5	Choose a healthy option when making a decision.
Standard 5.5.6	Describe the outcomes of a health-related decision.
Standard 6.	**Students will demonstrate the ability to use goal-setting skills to enhance health.**
Standard 6.5.1	Set a personal health goal and track progress toward its achievement.
Standard 6.5.2	Identify resources to assist in achieving a personal health goal.
Standard 7.	**Students will demonstrate the ability to practice health-enhancing behaviors and avoid or reduce health risks.**
Standard 7.5.1	Identify responsible personal health behaviors.
Standard 7.5.2	Demonstrate a variety of healthy practices and behaviors to maintain or improve personal health.
Standard 7.5.3	Demonstrate a variety of behaviors to avoid or reduce health risks.
Standard 8.	**Students will demonstrate the ability to advocate for personal, family, and community health.**
Standard 8.5.1	Express opinions and give accurate information about health issues.
Standard 8.5.2	Encourage others to make positive health choices.

Common Core State Standards Correlation

The activities included in *Healthy Habits for Healthy Kids (Grades 5 and up)* meet the following Common Core State Standards. For more information about these standards, go to *http://www.corestandards.org/* or visit *http://www.teachercreated.com/standards/* for activities related to each standard.

Reading: Informational Text
Key Ideas and Details
ELA.RI.5.1 Quote accurately from a text when explaining what the text says explicitly and when drawing inferences from the text.
ELA.RI.6.1 Cite textual evidence to support analysis of what the text says explicitly as well as inferences drawn from the text.
Craft and Structure
ELA.RI.5.4 Determine the meaning of general academic and domain-specific words and phrases in a text relevant *to a grade 5 topic or subject* area.
ELA.RI.6.4 Determine the meaning of words and phrases as they are used in a text including figurative, connotative, and technical meanings.
Integration of Knowledge and Ideas
ELA.RI.5.7 Draw on information from multiple print or digital sources, demonstrating the ability to locate an answer to a question quickly or to solve a problem efficiently.
ELA.RI.6.7 Integrate information presented in different media or formats (e.g., visually, quantitatively) as well as in words to develop a coherent understanding of a topic or issue.
Writing
Text Types and Purposes
ELA.W.5.1 Write opinion pieces on topics or texts, supporting a point of view with reasons and information.
ELA.W.6.1 Write arguments to support claims with clear reasons and relevant evidence.
ELA.W.6.2 Write informative/explanatory texts to examine a topic and convey ideas, concepts, and information through the selection, organization, and analysis of relevant content.
Research to Build and Present Knowledge
ELA.W.5.7 Conduct short research projects that use several sources to build knowledge through investigation of different aspects of a topic.
ELA.W.6.7 Conduct short research projects to answer a question drawing on several sources and refocusing the inquiry when appropriate.
Range of Writing
ELA.W. 5.10 Write routinely over extended time frames and shorter time frames for a range of discipline-specific tasks, purposes, and audiences.
ELA.W. 6.10 Write routinely over extended time frames and shorter time frames for a range of discipline-specific tasks, purposes, and audiences.
Speaking and Listening
Comprehension and Collaboration
ELA.SL.5.1 Engage effectively in a range of collaborative discussions with diverse partners *on grade 5 topics and texts*, building on others' ideas and expressing their own clearly.
ELA.SL.6.1 Engage effectively in a range of collaborative discussions with diverse partners *on grade 6 topics and texts and issues*, building on others' ideas and expressing their own clearly.
Language
Conventions of Standard English
ELA.L.5.1 Demonstrate command of the conventions of standard English grammar and usage when writing or speaking.
ELA.L.6.1 Demonstrate command of the conventions of standard English grammar and usage when writing or speaking.
Vocabulary Acquisition and Use
ELA.L.5.4 Determine or clarify the meaning of unknown and multiple-meaning words and phrases based on grade 5 reading and content, choosing flexibly from a range of strategies.
ELA.L.6.4 Determine or clarify the meaning of unknown and multiple-meaning words and phrases based on grade 6 reading and content, choosing flexibly from a range of strategies.
ELA.L.6.6 Acquire and use accurately grade-appropriate general academic and domain-specific words and phrases; gather vocabulary knowledge when considering a word or phrase important to comprehension or expression.

Take the Pledge

Directions: Read and practice the "Healthy Habits Pledge." When you are ready, recite it to a friend or family member. Sign your name at the bottom of the pledge when you have completed this activity, and bring the page back to school.

Healthy Habits Pledge

I pledge to stay healthy and clean
through exercise and good hygiene.
I will eat balanced meals every day
to have more energy to learn and to play.
Every night I will get a good rest
to be more ready to do my best.
If I work hard to be healthy and strong
I'll be happier my whole life long.

I, ______________________________, have read and learned the Healthy Habits Pledge.

Directions: Write at least one personal health goal you would like to try this week. Choose from the following ideas. Later, as you learn more about healthy food choices and healthy habits, you may wish to write a goal more specific to your health needs.

- Choose servings the size of your fist.
- Have fruits and vegetables on half of your plate.
- Enjoy water as your favorite drink.
- Eat foods from each food group.
- Choose foods with less sugar and fat.

Week ______________________________	Met	Not Yet
My personal goal this week is to ______________________________ ______________________________.		

Challenge: Continue setting goals for yourself each week. Use the "Personal Health Goals" page in your journal to keep track.

Name

What Makes a Healthy Food?

Why do we call some foods "healthy" foods? What makes these foods better for us than others?

For thousands of years people have made a connection between what we eat and how we feel. Interest in many fruits and vegetables developed because people believed that they provided specific medicinal, or health, benefits. We still see this today. Scientists have learned which foods contain specific nutrients. For example, fish provides us with protein, vitamins, and minerals. These nutrients are needed for growth and to maintain healthy bodies. Scientists study how different nutrients increase overall good health. Often, these nutrients are listed on a food's packaging so that we can make good food choices.

We are going to learn more about healthy foods. Healthy foods have a good balance of nutrients and calories. That is, from the amount of calories you eat, you're getting nutrients that help your body. Our bodies use the calories and nutrients we eat for energy and to grow.

Nutrients we need include protein, vitamins, and minerals. Vitamins and minerals help our cells, tissues, and organs develop and stay healthy. Nutrients also help us fight disease and heal when we are injured.

It is important to remember that "empty calories" do not give us as many nutrients. Foods with a lot of sugar or fat often have more empty calories but fewer vitamins and minerals. Empty calories are found in foods with added sugar like sodas or extra salt like French fries or potato chips. These foods are treats, or "sometimes" foods, and should be enjoyed in small amounts. Sometimes foods do not give us the nutrients we need to be healthy, strong, and energized.

Always Foods	Sometimes Foods
fruit vegetables	chips cookies

Directions: Write your ideas about healthy foods in the web below. Combine your ideas with classmates, to create a class web.

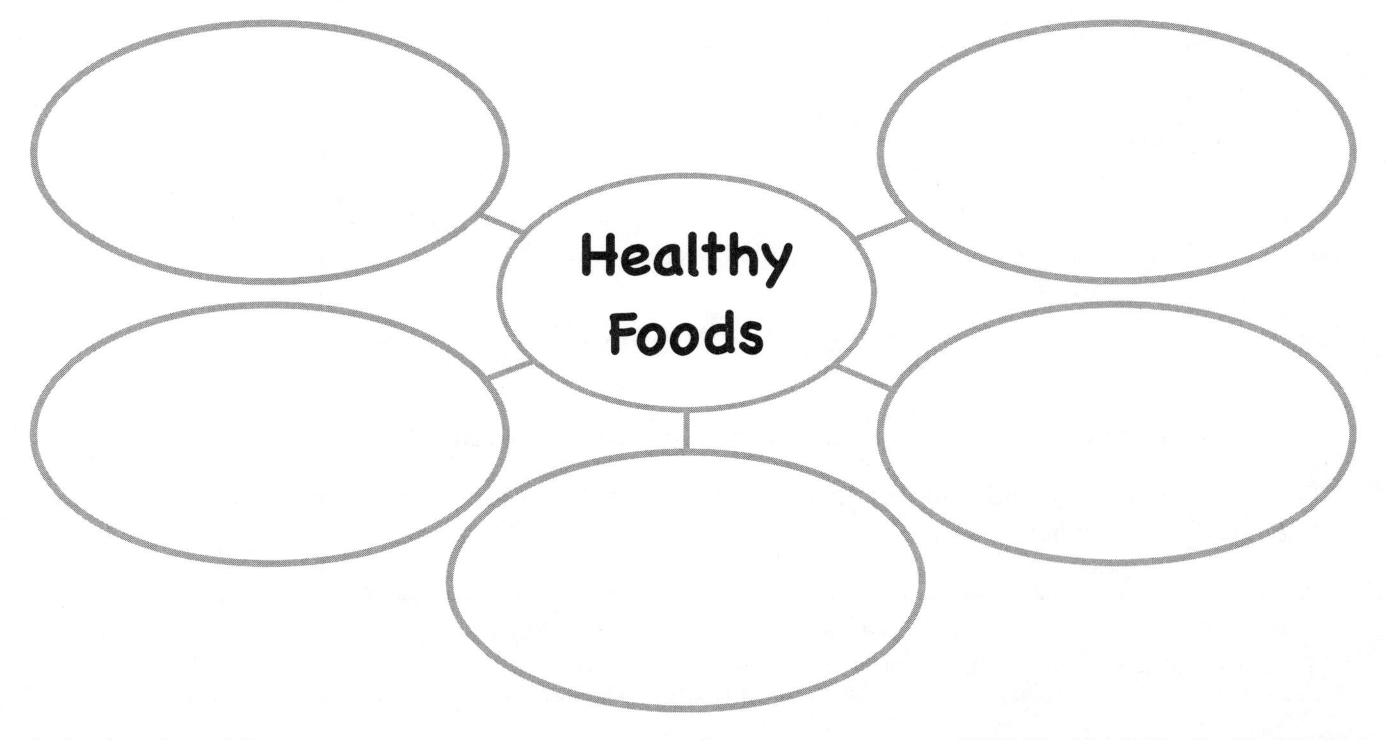

Name

Healthy Foods Come in Groups

We need to eat a variety of foods to make sure we get the different nutrients that our bodies need. One way to think about this is to categorize the foods we eat into five groups. The My Plate diagram shows these five food groups. This picture can help us remember how much of our total food should come from each group. We may have more of one food group or another at one meal, but this visual can help us think about what we eat over the course of each day.

1. What are some of your current favorite foods in each group? Write your answers on the diagram.

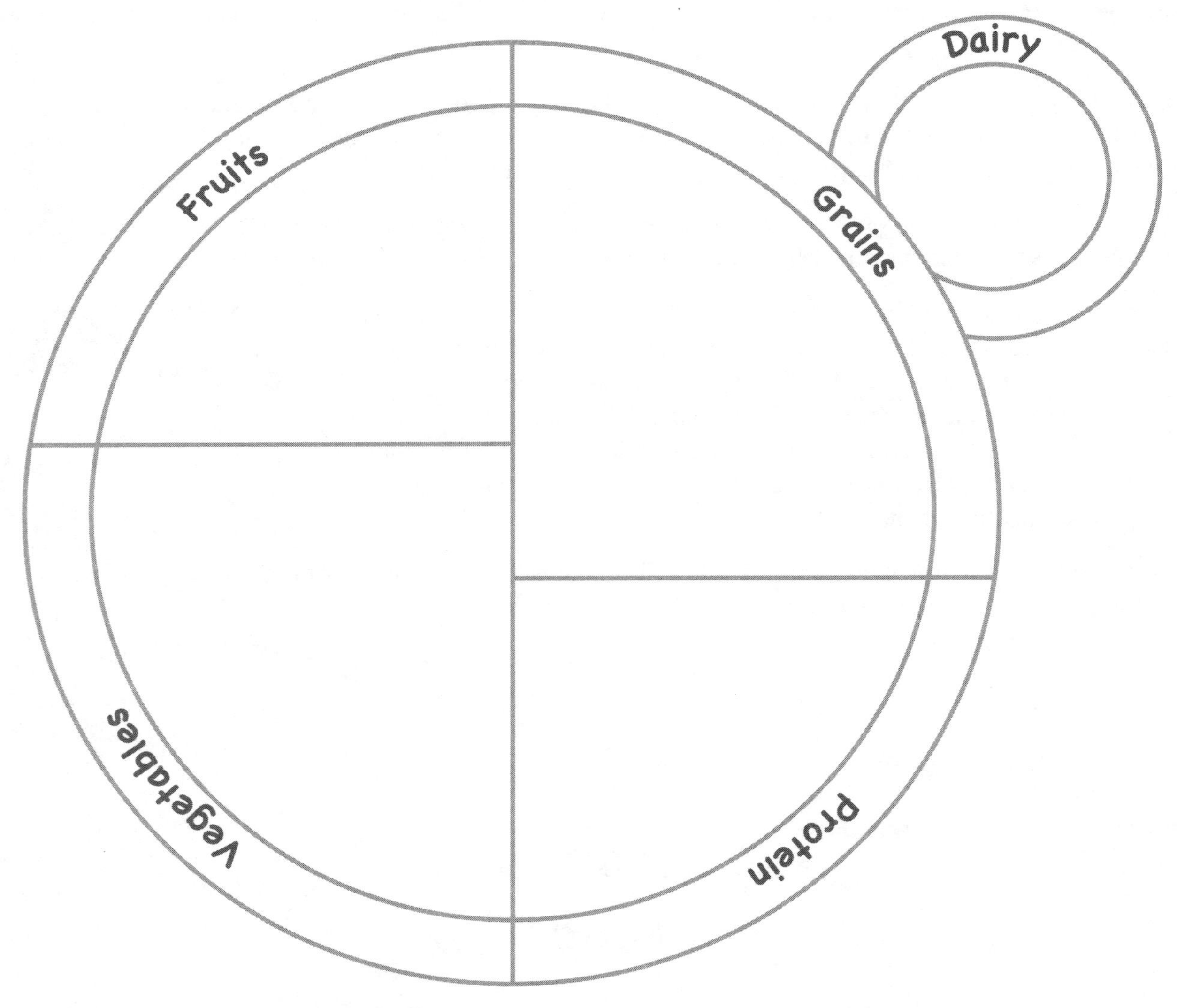

2. Do you think you are getting enough of each food group? **YES NO**

3. Talk to a classmate and compare "plates." Add one idea for each food group from a classmate's plate. Circle the new ideas.

Teacher Note: The outline above is based on the USDA My Plate graphic. See pages 4 and 5 for more information on this informative USDA site.

Name

Exercise for a Healthier Life

We know that eating right and getting exercise are important for healthy minds and bodies. Different types of exercise help us in different ways. Deep breathing, stretching, and balancing exercises can help us relax our bodies and focus our minds. Isometric and aerobic-type exercises help keep us in shape by building and toning muscles and increasing our endurance. Here are some examples of the different types of exercises. You might do one or two to start the day or to take a break from studies.

Challenge yourself. As you improve, increase the amount of time you do each one. Remember though, it is more important to do them correctly to protect your muscles and joints than it is to do them fast! As a group, be respectful of each other. Agree that each person will focus on his or her own movements. No one will tease or bother anyone else.

Breathing Techniques: Steady breathing can help you calm down and be more relaxed. Practicing breathing techniques can help you in a variety of situations, and it is easy. Plus, you can alter your breathing anytime, anywhere. Try these techniques:

- ☐ Close your eyes and inhale air as deep into your lungs as you can. Think about where the air is going. Be aware of your lungs as they expand. Breathe out as much air as you can, keeping each breath steady.
- ☐ Breathe in for the count of four. Hold the breath for the count of four. Breathe out for the count of four. Try not to take another breath for the count of four. Then, try breathing in and out for a count of 5, then 6, etc.
- ☐ Breathe in through your nose. Breathe out through your mouth, quietly saying "haaa." Focus on "breathing out." Your body will do the "breathing in" for you.
- ☐ Lie on your belly. Breathe in. Relax as you breathe out. Bend your knees and hold your ankles behind you. Breathe in and lift your head, chest, and legs off the floor. Lift your head and feet towards the ceiling to stretch. Breathe out as you come back down to the floor.
- ☐ Tense and relax one part of your body at a time. Begin with your toes, tightening them and then relaxing. Take a deep breath as you relax. Continue with your legs, arms, chest, and neck. Take deep breaths as you release each muscle group.

Isometric Exercises: Isometrics are a type of strength training you can do sitting in a chair!

- ☐ Sit on a chair that has a back or sit on a mat next to a wall. Place your hands to your sides. Pull your stomach in hard against the backrest. Hold for 10 seconds, release, and repeat.
- ☐ Sit on your chair. Put your thumb and palm of your hands on the chair. Push to raise yourself completely off the chair. Hold for 5–10 seconds, lower, and repeat.
- ☐ Sit on your chair. Bend forward and hold your toes. Pull upward with your back while holding your toes. Can you feel your back arching and stretching? Repeat this exercise a few times to loosen up.
- ☐ Sit straight up on your chair with your arms hanging loosely at your sides. Raise one leg straight out in front of you and hold for 5 seconds. Repeat with the other leg. Can you do this for a minute? Can you do it longer?

Name

Exercise for a Healthier Life *(cont.)*

Stretching Exercises help us stay flexible. Flexibility enables us to bend and have full range of motion. A stretch should be noticeable, but never painful. Treat your body with respect and don't try to do what your neighbor is doing. Do a stretch that feels good for your own body. We are not all flexible in the same ways. With practice, you may stretch farther, but you may not. The goal of these exercises is to help you relax and focus on your work.

- ☐ Sit with one leg extended. Bend the other leg in so that your foot touches the extended leg. Bend forward from your waist and touch your toes with both hands.
- ☐ Stand behind your chair and rest your hands lightly on the chair back. Raise up on your toes, hold, and lower down on your toes to stretch your calves.
- ☐ Assume a position on all fours, relaxed and looking at the floor. Breathe in, lower your stomach (arching your back downward), and raise your head and look up. Then breathe out and lift your stomach, arching your back, and looking down.
- ☐ Stand straight and lift your arms over your head. Remember to drop your shoulders down away from your neck so they are not scrunched up. Reach as high as you can. Focus on the different muscles in your body. Can you feel your shoulders release and your sides stretch (lengthen)? What about your leg muscles? Did you feel them tense and release?

Balance Training is communication between your mind and your muscles. Balance training is important at any age. It is important in almost every sport because as you move, you change your center of gravity. For some of us, it is easy, but for others, it can take some practice. Try these:

- ☐ Balance on one foot for 30 seconds. Hold the other leg up straight in front or with a bent knee. Then, balance on the other foot. Switch back and forth a few times. Is it easier for you on one side than the other?
- ☐ Raise up on tiptoes with your hands overhead and hold for 30 seconds. Lower down, and repeat. If you can balance easily, try it again with your eyes closed.
- ☐ Walk on a straight line (tape or a line on the floor) for 20 paces. Try walking with your hands in different positions—stretched out from your sides, over your head, or straight down.

Aerobic, or cardio-type exercises, help build endurance. Generally they are done for extended periods of time, but you can start with these simple activities. Set a timer or watch the clock. Try these exercises for one minute to start. As endurance improves, increase the amount of time you do each one.

- ☐ Jog in place.
- ☐ March and swing your arms.
- ☐ Do jumping-jacks.
- ☐ Jump forward two jumps and back one jump. Do this around the classroom as space allows.
- ☐ Hold your arms out (shoulder height) and do arm circles. Try small circles, then larger ones.
- ☐ Stretch and reach overhead. Then, bend to one side. Reach up again and then bend to the other side. Repeat.
- ☐ Hop as many times as you can on one foot. Switch and hop on the other foot.

Name

Think About Fruit

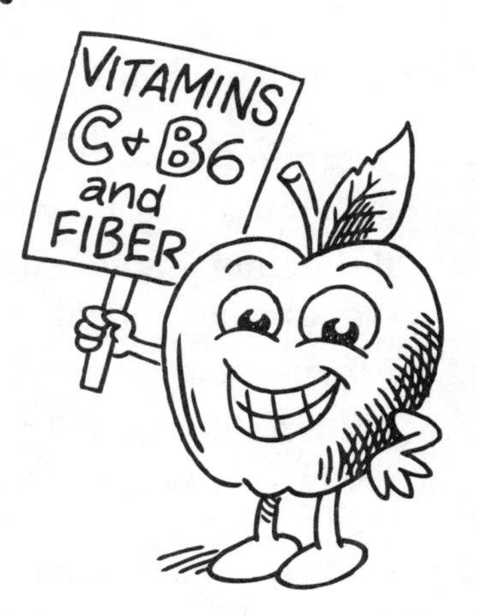

Fruit is one of the healthy food groups. We define *fruit* as the sweet, fleshy part of a plant that has the seed or seeds of the plant. It may be sweet or sour and is usually edible in its raw state. Eating fruit helps keep our hearts healthy. A healthy heart pumps blood through the body effectively. Healthy foods such as fruits also lower the risk of disease, such as cancer and diabetes.

Directions: Here is a list of different fruits. Did you know there were so many? Check the boxes of all the fruits you have eaten. Circle three fruits you would like to try.

Fruits

- ☐ apples
- ☐ apricots
- ☐ bananas
- ☐ blackberries
- ☐ blueberries
- ☐ breadfruit
- ☐ cantaloupe
- ☐ cherimoya
- ☐ cherries
- ☐ clementines
- ☐ coconut
- ☐ cranberries
- ☐ Crenshaw melon
- ☐ dragon fruit
- ☐ figs
- ☐ grapefruit
- ☐ grapes
- ☐ guava
- ☐ honeydew
- ☐ huckleberries
- ☐ kiwi fruit
- ☐ kumquat
- ☐ lemons
- ☐ limes
- ☐ loquat
- ☐ mangoes
- ☐ nectarines
- ☐ oranges
- ☐ papayas
- ☐ passion fruit
- ☐ peaches
- ☐ pears
- ☐ persimmon
- ☐ pineapples
- ☐ plums
- ☐ pomegranate
- ☐ quince
- ☐ raisins
- ☐ raspberries
- ☐ strawberries
- ☐ tangerines
- ☐ watermelon

Challenge: Choose one of the fruits you have an interest in trying. Do some research to find out more about this healthy food. Add your information to your "New Healthy Foods" page (page 82) in your journal.

Name

Think About Fruit *(cont.)*

Fruit has many vitamins and other nutrients, including the following:

Vitamin C—Most fruit is high in fiber and vitamin C. Vitamin C helps our bodies heal if we get a cut. It helps tissues inside our bodies heal, too. It helps us have strong bones and teeth.

Potassium—Some fruits are high in potassium. Potassium helps our nerves and muscles function the way they should. It helps our heart beat properly.

Fiber—Fiber helps us digest our food so our bodies can use it for energy.

Folic Acid—Many fruits also have folic acid. It is a type of B vitamin. It helps our bodies make red blood cells. Red blood cells carry oxygen from our lungs to all parts of our body.

Directions: Answer the following questions.

1. Bananas are a good source of potassium. Potassium helps my ________________________ and ________________________ work well.

2. Apples, berries, and figs are good sources of fiber. Fiber helps digest foods to give me ________________________ .

3. Oranges and grapefruit are a good source of folic acid, which makes red ________________________ ________________________.

4. Red blood cells carry oxygen from our ________________________ to all parts of our body.

Challenge: Create a recipe for a fruit salad. Which five fruits would you mix together? What vitamins and nutrients would your salad provide? Use a journal page to share your recipe and nutritional information.

____

____

____

____

____

Name

Growing Fruit

If I plant an apple seed, will I have apples to eat? Maybe you will, if you live in the right climate, and if you take care of the plant. Still, it will take a long time for the tree to grow and give fruit. Some fruits are easier and faster to grow at home in a garden than fruit trees. Strawberries, raspberries, and blueberries grow well in a garden setting. They are often planted from nursery "starts" instead of seeds. Each of these fruits is a tasty way to get vitamin C and fiber.

You might have a fruit tree in your yard. You might live near a farmers' market and be able to choose from a variety of fresh fruits. You can buy bananas at the grocery store. Each of these provides options for enjoying a variety of fresh fruit that's good for us.

Directions: Research to learn about fruits that grow in your area. Use the chart to organize your notes. Find out:

1. Which fruits could you grow at home in a backyard garden or in a container garden? ____________

   ____

2. Which local fruits might you get fresh at a farmers' market? ____________

   ____

3. Which fruits do not grow locally that you would have to find at a grocery store? ____________

   ____

Backyard Fruits	Local Farm Fruits	Fruits from the Store
____________	____________	____________
____________	____________	____________
____________	____________	____________
____________	____________	____________
____________	____________	____________
____________	____________	____________

Name

Stone Fruits

Fruits have seeds, pits, or stones inside. "Stone fruits" have one very large, hard seed. They grow best in warmer climates and can be damaged by severe winter temperatures. They bloom early in the spring, with fruit ready for harvest from May through September. Here are four examples of stone fruits:

Apricot **Growing Season** May–August	**Vitamins:** Good source of vitamins A and C **Nutrients:** High in fiber and potassium **Producers:** Turkey and Iran are the top two producing countries. Most apricots grown in the United States are from California and Washington. **Fact:** Less than one quarter of apricots grown are sold fresh. Most are sold as dried fruits.
Cherry **Growing Season** May–July	**Vitamin:** Good source of vitamin C **Nutrients:** High in fiber, potassium, and iron; contains traces of boron, a mineral that helps maintain bone health. **Producers:** Turkey is the leading producer of cherries; the United States is second. Most U.S. cherries are grown in Michigan, then California, Oregon, and Washington. **Types:** There are two main types—sweet cherries and tart cherries. **Fact:** Cherry trees are also known for their beautiful blossoms.
Peach **Growing Season** June–August	**Vitamins:** Good source of vitamins A and C **Nutrients:** High in fiber and potassium **Producers:** China is the number one producer of peaches and Italy is the second. Most peaches grown in United States are from California, South Carolina, and Georgia. **Types:** There are two main types—clingstone and freestone. **Facts:** The flesh sticks to the stone in clingstone peaches. The stone easily separates from the flesh in freestone peaches.
Plum **Growing Season** May–November	**Vitamins:** Good source of vitamins A and C **Nutrients:** High in fiber, potassium, iron, calcium, and magnesium **Producers:** China is the leading producer and the United States is second. Most plums grown in the United States are from California. **Facts:** Dried plums are called prunes. Plums harvested for eating must be picked by hand. Plums that will be dried as prunes are machine harvested.

Directions: Use the information about stone fruits to answer the questions below or on the back of the page.

1. Which fruit has the longest growing season? ______________________________

2. A trace mineral that helps keep bones healthy can be found in ______________________.

   This mineral is called ______________________________________.

3. What are some differences between peaches and apricots? ______________________________

   ____

4. Which characteristics do these fruits have in common? ______________________________

Name

How Well Do You Know Melons?

In general, melons are good sources of vitamins A, B6, and C. Vitamin B6 helps our bodies convert food into energy. Melons also provide nutrients, including potassium, folate, and niacin, depending on the type. Melons come in different colors and have different types of skin or rinds. Some are smooth and some are rough or "netted." The blossom end smells fruity on some of these melons when they are ripe.

Directions: Match each melon to its description. Write the correct letter next to the name of each melon.

1. **Casaba** ________
2. **Crenshaw** ________
3. **Honeydew** ________
4. **Musk melon** ________
5. **Persian** ________
6. **Watermelon** ________

A. -large, round
-heavily netted
-light green rind turns tan when ripe
-coral-colored flesh

B. -round or oval-shaped
-netted rind with light ribbing
-light-green rind turns tan when ripe
-salmon-colored flesh

C. -rounded shape
-a point at stem end
-no netting
-hard-ridged, thick rind
-irregular, shallow furrows end to end
-golden-yellow rind with hint of green
-creamy, pale green flesh

D. -round or oval shape
-light green, gray green, or dark green rind
-often has contrasting stripes
-red, yellow, orange, or white flesh

E. -smooth
-white to greenish rind
-green or white flesh

F. -teardrop shape
-rough rind with no netting
-yellow and green to golden-yellow rind
-peach-colored flesh

The true cantaloupe, a hard-shelled melon, is rarely grown in this country. True cantaloupes are grown mostly in the Mediterranean. They don't have an orderly "netting," and the ribs are heavier and more deeply grooved. What we call a cantaloupe is really a "musk melon." The melons we see are related to pumpkins, squash, gourds, and cucumbers.

Name

Dragon Fruit

1. What is your first impression of this fruit? ____________________

____

Describe it. ____________________

____

2. Would you like to try it? ____________________

Why or why not? ____________________

____

3. What do you think it tastes like? ____________________

____

Have you seen a strange-looking fruit at the grocery store lately with an even stranger name? The appearance of this unusual fruit may have inspired its common name—dragon fruit. Known as pitaya or pitahaya in South America and Asia, it's from the cactus family. The climbing cactus vine is native to Mexico and Central and South America. The football-shaped fruit has leathery, leafy skin. It is usually dark red, but may be pink or yellow. The sweet tasting flesh is red, white, or yellow, with hundreds of tiny black seeds. Many people like to scoop the chilled fruit out of the center with a spoon. It tastes like a cross between a kiwi and a watermelon.

Dragon fruit has a long growing season, lasting from June to December. It does well in tropical climates. Dragon fruit requires pollination, but the flowers bloom only at night. In native areas, bats and moths take care of pollination. Growers in some areas have to go out in the fields and pollinate by hand. A plant may flower four to six times in a year.

Dragon fruit is high in fiber and the seeds contain omega-3 fatty acids. As with many fruits, dragon fruit is high in vitamin C. It also is a good source of B vitamins, iron, calcium, and phosphorus.

4. What would you say to a friend or family member to encourage that person to try dragon fruit?

____

____

5. What are some ways you might eat dragon fruit?

____

____

Challenge: Research and learn about one other fruit that is new to you. Design a mini-poster to present the fruit to your classmates. Remember, a mini-poster should have an illustration and facts or information presented in an interesting way to catch people's attention.
Here are some suggestions: ***cherimoya, kumquat, persimmon,*** or ***pomelo.***

Name

Bunches of Bananas

Ever wondered about the different bananas in the produce section? There are red ones, green ones, and yellow ones. Some are long and some are short. Here is a summary of some varieties:

Yellow Bananas: The most common type of yellow banana sold in stores is the Cavendish. They average seven inches long, with a yellow peel that develops brown spots as it ripens. The pale, creamy flesh has a sweet flavor we identify as "banana." People have their own preferences for how ripe they like bananas. Most people eat Cavendish bananas fresh or use them when baking. These bananas grow in South and Central America. Yellow bananas are a good source of potassium. They are also high in vitamin C, fiber, and iron. This type of banana has the lowest amount of natural sugar.

Red Bananas: The dark red peel of red bananas makes the flesh a slightly pink color. Some people think this smaller, plump banana has a hint of raspberry taste. These bananas should be eaten only when ripe. People eat them fresh, use them in baking, and cook them in pork or chicken with other seasonings. Native to India, they also grow in South and Central America. Their nutrient value is similar to other varieties of bananas. They are high in vitamins C and B6, fiber, potassium, and iron.

Manzanos: Manzano bananas are called "apple bananas." These small bananas are about four inches long. They have a yellow peel that darkens as they ripen. The flesh is about the same color as the bananas you are probably used to eating. Some people say it is crunchy, with a hint of apple flavor. It's better to eat this fruit when it's ripe, appearing dark yellow with black spots. Manzano bananas can be eaten fresh, used in baking, or fried. They grow in South and Central America as well as Africa. They are high in Vitamin C, fiber, and iron.

Directions: Fill in the chart below with information on the three types of bananas.

Type of Banana	Yellow 	Red 	Manzano 
Appearance			
Vitamins			
Nutrients			
Flavors			
How to Eat			
Grown in			

A Word About Plantains: Plantains are members of the banana family, but they're not bananas. They are starchy, not sweet, with a consistency like a potato. We eat this fruit cooked, as it is inedible raw. Plantains may have green, yellow, or black peels that are thicker than banana peels. The fruit inside is yellow or pink. The darker the peel, the sweeter the plantain tastes. You can cook and eat them at any state of ripeness. They continue to ripen over time. Plantains are sold individually, not in a bunch. People fry, grill, or bake plantains to eat them. This fruit is native to India and grows in other tropical countries as well. Plantains are high in vitamins A and C, fiber, potassium, and iron.

Challenge: Give three reasons why plantains are different from bananas. Use the back of this page.

Name

Think About Vegetables

There are different categories of vegetables. Eating vegetables from each sub-group helps us get the variety of vitamins and minerals we need to be healthy.

Directions: Check the boxes of the vegetables you have eaten on pages 20 and 21. Fill in the boxes for vegetables you have never heard of. Choose one of these new vegetables to research. Add your findings to your "New Healthy Foods" journal page on page 82.

Dark Green Leafy Vegetables

- ☐ arugula
- ☐ beet greens
- ☐ bok choy
- ☐ broccoli
- ☐ broccolini
- ☐ chicory
- ☐ Chinese cabbage
- ☐ cilantro
- ☐ collard greens
- ☐ endive
- ☐ escarole
- ☐ kale
- ☐ leaf lettuce, red and green
- ☐ mustard greens
- ☐ parsley
- ☐ romaine lettuce
- ☐ spinach
- ☐ swiss chard
- ☐ turnip greens
- ☐ watercress

Red and Orange Vegetables

- ☐ carrots
- ☐ orange bell peppers *
- ☐ pimientos
- ☐ pumpkin *
- ☐ red bell peppers *
- ☐ red chili peppers *
- ☐ sweet potatoes
- ☐ tomatoes *
- ☐ winter squash *
- ☐ yams

* These culinary or fruit vegetables have seeds inside like fruit but are often cooked and served like vegetables.

Beans and Peas (Legumes)

- ☐ black beans
- ☐ black-eyed peas, dried
- ☐ cowpeas, dried
- ☐ fava beans
- ☐ garbanzo beans
- ☐ Great Northern beans
- ☐ kidney beans
- ☐ lentils
- ☐ mature lima beans
- ☐ mung beans
- ☐ navy beans
- ☐ pink beans
- ☐ pinto beans
- ☐ red beans
- ☐ soy beans/edamame
- ☐ split peas
- ☐ white beans

Name

Think About Vegetables *(cont.)*

Starchy Vegetables

- [ ] black-eyed peas, fresh
- [ ] corn
- [ ] green peas
- [ ] jicama
- [ ] green lima beans
- [ ] parsnips
- [ ] pigeon peas
- [ ] plantains
- [ ] potatoes
- [ ] taro
- [ ] water chestnuts

Other Vegetables

- [ ] artichoke
- [ ] asparagus
- [ ] avocado *
- [ ] bamboo shoots
- [ ] bean sprouts, cooked
- [ ] green beans
- [ ] yellow beans
- [ ] beets
- [ ] Brussels sprouts
- [ ] cabbage
- [ ] cauliflower
- [ ] celery
- [ ] chives
- [ ] cucumbers *
- [ ] daikon
- [ ] eggplant *
- [ ] fennel
- [ ] garlic
- [ ] horseradish
- [ ] iceberg lettuce
- [ ] kohlrabi
- [ ] leeks
- [ ] mushrooms
- [ ] okra *
- [ ] olives *
- [ ] onion
- [ ] green chile pepper *
- [ ] green bell pepper *
- [ ] purple bell pepper *
- [ ] yellow bell pepper *
- [ ] pickles (cucumber)
- [ ] radish
- [ ] romanesco
- [ ] rhubarb
- [ ] shallots
- [ ] snap peas
- [ ] snow peas
- [ ] tomatillo
- [ ] turnip
- [ ] wax beans
- [ ] yellow summer squash
- [ ] zucchini

* These culinary or fruit vegetables have seeds inside like fruit but are often cooked and served like vegetables.

Salad 1—List the vegetables you usually have when you eat a salad. ______________________________

____

Salad 2—Now, create a list of salad ingredients by picking one item from each of the five vegetable sections. ____

____

Which salad has more variety? **Salad 1** ____________ or **Salad 2** ____________

Name

Different Kinds of Vegetables

We all know we need to eat vegetables and there are so many different kinds! They are healthy foods that provide us with important vitamins and other nutrients, including:

- **Vitamin A** keeps our eyes and skin healthy and helps to prevent infections.
- **Vitamin C** helps our bodies build strong bones and teeth.
- **Folic acid** helps our bodies make new red blood cells to carry oxygen to all parts of our bodies.
- **Fiber** works to digest the other foods we eat. Fiber helps lower cholesterol and helps prevent heart disease.

Directions: Review the list of different vegetables on pages 20–21. Research a vegetable from each section. Write what you learn about these new vegetables. Circle the part of each vegetable that you can eat.

Vegetable: ____________________ **Part you eat:** root stem leaf flower

Vitamins: ____

Nutrients: ____

Vegetable: ____________________ **Part you eat:** root stem leaf flower

Vitamins: ____

Nutrients: ____

Vegetable: ____________________ **Part you eat:** root stem leaf flower

Vitamins: ____

Nutrients: ____

Vegetable: ____________________ **Part you eat:** root stem leaf flower

Vitamins: ____

Nutrients: ____

Vegetable: ____________________ **Part you eat:** root stem leaf flower

Vitamins: ____

Nutrients: ____

Name

Culinary Vegetables Crossword

Culinary vegetables are foods that scientists say are fruits because they have seeds inside. We call them "culinary vegetables" or sometimes "fruit vegetables" because we prepare and eat them as vegetables. We eat them in salads with other vegetables or we cook them with savory seasonings.

Directions: Solve the clues for each culinary vegetable. Then, use the answers to complete the crossword puzzle on the following page.

Across

1. An ____________________________ comes in different colors and sizes but is most known for being purple. Scientists think of it as a large berry. It doesn't really look like its name.

4. Many people roast and eat ____________________________ seeds, as well as cook and eat the fruit, especially in the fall. It also makes a great decoration.

5. We use a ____________________________, a nutrient-rich food, in salads and to make sauces and other foods. Some varieties are the size of a grape and others can be the size of a fist.

7. Related to watermelons and pumpkins, a ____________________________ is surprisingly nutrient-rich. People eat this fruit vegetable with the waxy green skin raw or pickled.

8. There are winter and summer varieties of ____________________________. They grow in all sizes and shapes. They can be green, yellow, reddish orange, orange or combinations of these colors.

9. ____________________________ trees are not harvested for the first 15 years. We also use the oil from this culinary vegetable in cooking.

Down

2. ____________________________ come in almost every color of the rainbow: green, yellow, orange, red, purple, and brown.

3. An ____________________________ grows on a tall evergreen tree and has more potassium than a banana. This fruit vegetable has the nickname "alligator pear."

6. ____________________________ is a small green food with more vitamins and minerals than you can imagine. It's often thought of as a Southern food. Some people call this fruit vegetable "lady fingers." Can you guess why?____

Culinary or Fruit Vegetables

avocado	okra	pumpkin
cucumber	olive	squash
eggplant	peppers	tomato

Name

Culinary Vegetables Crossword *(cont.)*

Directions: Use the answers to the clues on page 23 to fill in the crossword puzzle. Then answer the questions below it.

1 2 3 4 5 6 7 8 9

1. What is a culinary vegetable? ______________________________

____

2. What is another name for culinary vegetable? ______________________________

3. Which culinary vegetable can you use to make dip, eat sliced, or add to a salad?

____

4. Which culinary vegetable grows on a tree and can be green or black?

____

5. Squash are culinary vegetables. Name a type of squash that can be decorated for a holiday celebration.

____

6. Which culinary vegetable is used to make pickles? ______________________________

Name

Peppers

Peppers are a type of culinary vegetable—they have seeds on the inside. They provide us with vitamins A, B6, and C. Peppers are also a good source of fiber. The peppers we eat are not related to black pepper, which is ground and used as a spice to season foods.

Are peppers sweet or spicy? It depends on the variety. Some peppers lack the gene that makes *capsaicin*, the chemical that makes peppers taste spicy or hot. This chemical causes the mouth to feel a burning sensation. It tells your body the temperature is rising, and your mouth feels as if it's on fire!

Sweet Peppers

The most common variety of sweet pepper is a bell pepper. Green bell peppers turn red as they ripen. Sweet peppers have a mild flavor and varying amounts of sweetness depending on the variety. Other pepper varieties are green, purple, or yellow when not fully ripe and turn orange, red, black, or chocolate brown as they ripen. There are sweet banana peppers, sweet cherry peppers, and Cubanelle sweet peppers. What do you think a sweet banana pepper looks like? Sweet cherry peppers are slightly spicy and look like a small red bell pepper. Cubanelle peppers are long and thin. They are pale yellow-green and turn red when fully ripe. However, they're most often sold unripe to be used as a spice or roasted. Pepperoncini, sometimes known as Tuscan peppers are mild and are often sold pickled. People eat sweet peppers raw in salads, as a crunchy veggie, or cooked.

bell pepper

banana pepper

cherry pepper

Cubanelle

pepperoncini

Spicy (Hot) Peppers

People use chili peppers, or spicy peppers, to season other foods. Some types of chili peppers include jalapeños; red or green Fresno chilies; serrano, Anaheim, and habañero chilies.

Chili peppers are rated on a scale for heat. This scale is called the Scoville Heat Unit Scale. Scientists dilute a pepper in sugar water. They keep adding sugar until the pepper does not taste hot any more. The more sugar needed, the hotter the pepper ranks on the scale. Bell peppers rate a zero. A jalapeño pepper may rate between 2,500 and 8,000 units on the scale. Very hot habañero chilies rate between 200,000 and 300,000 units. Be careful not to burn your mouth!

You may have seen a shiny green jalapeño. Red Fresno chilies are similar to jalapeños. They work well in salsa. A milder green Fresno chili can be found in the summer, but it doesn't dry as well. Serrano chilies are smaller and hotter than jalapeños. Anaheim chilies are green when fresh and turn red when dried. They may be mild or very hot. Habañero chilies are green and ripen to orange or red. They are much hotter than jalapeños.

serrano chili

Anaheim chili

Fresno chili

jalapeño

habañero

Name

Peppers *(cont.)*

1. Use the chart below to organize the information you read on page 25. Write facts you have learned about each type of pepper on the chart.
2. Research to find out more about a type of pepper that interests you. You might also want to research the Scoville Heat Unit Scale for more information. Add the data from your research to your chart.

Name of Pepper	Mild or Spicy	Characteristics

3. Which types of peppers have you eaten? ______________________________

____

4. What is your favorite way to eat peppers? ______________________________

____

5. Which pepper would you like to try?______________________________

Why? ____

Name

Vegetable Family Tree

Some of the vegetables we eat belong to the same plant family. If we like one vegetable in the family, we might enjoy another food from the same family. This can be a way to try new foods.

The *Apiacea* plant family is interesting because some of the foods are used as vegetables and some are used as herbs, or seasonings, for other foods. Most members of this plant family grow in northern, temperate regions. The plants have feathery leaves.

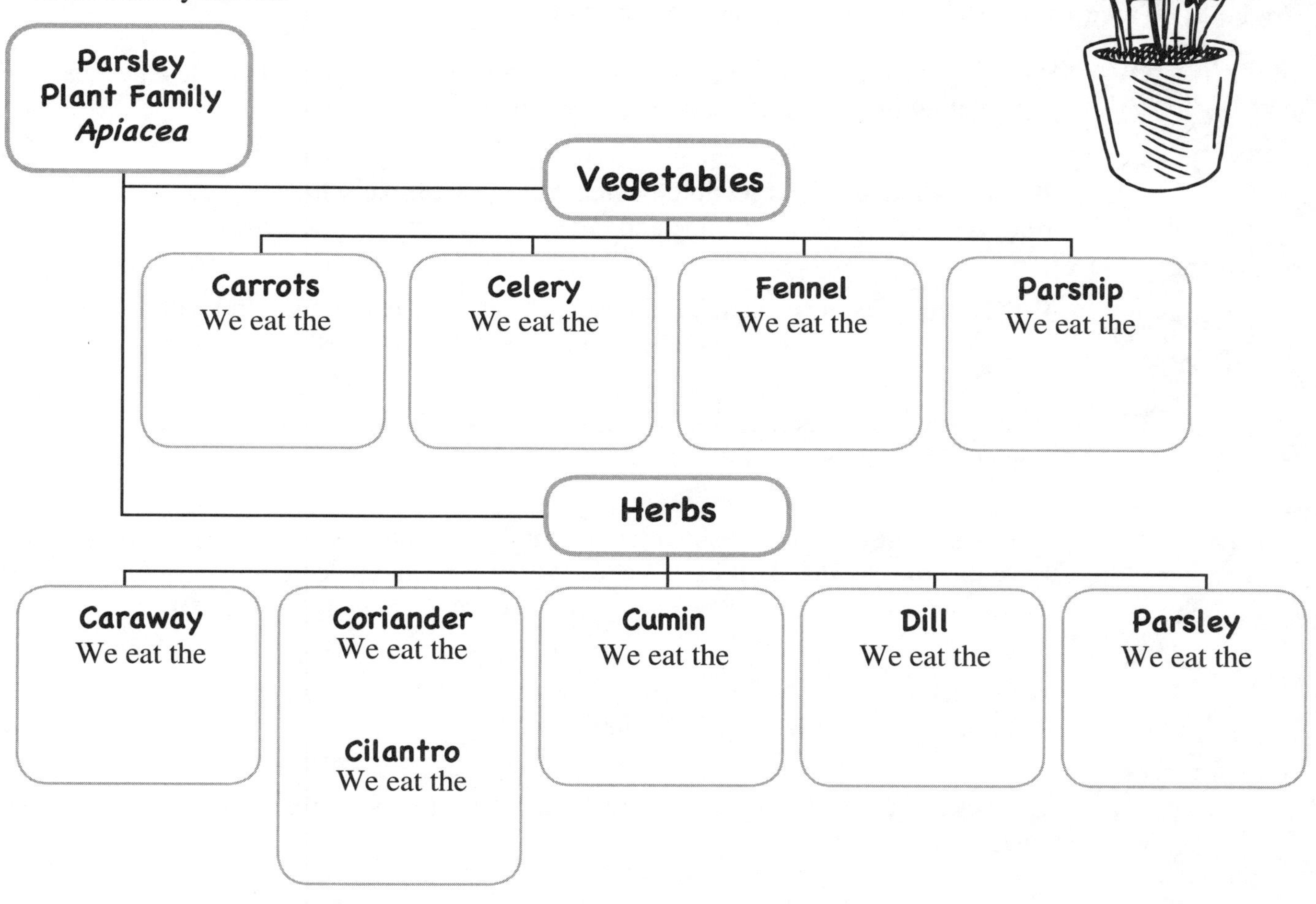

1. Foods we eat from the parsley plant family include the *roots*, *stems*, *seeds*, and *leaves* of the plants. In the spaces provided, identify which part of each vegetable or herb is eaten.
2. Research a food from this family. Share an interesting fact. ______________________________

   ____

   This food is rich in nutrients such as: ______________________________
3. Which two foods would you like to try? ________________ ________________

Extension: Find another plant family to investigate, for example the "nightshade" family or *Brassicaceae* (formerly *Cruciferae* family). Create a chart similar to the one above. Work with classmates to combine information about foods in this plant family to fill in the diagram.

Name

All Kinds of Squash

Squash are culinary vegetables. There are two main types—summer and winter. Both types grow in warm weather, but summer squash is sensitive to frost. The summer fruits grow on bushes instead of vines and should be harvested before fully ripe for best flavor. Summer squash varieties include yellow squash and zucchini. Most winter squash grows on vines and is harvested when the fruit is fully mature. Mature fruit develops a hard skin and is a solid color. The seeds are also fully mature. Squash stores well in cool, dry conditions. There is a sub-group of winter squash that doesn't keep quite as well. Acorn squash and spaghetti squash are in this group and can be identified by the ridges or stripes (or both) on their skins. Here are some common varieties of squash:

Acorn squash has harvest green skin speckled with orange patches. The flesh is pale yellow-orange. It has a unique flavor that is sweet and nutty.

Banana squash is a large, oblong-shaped squash. It has a thick salmon-colored rind. The dense flesh is orange and tastes rich and sweet when cooked.

Buttercup squash is a squat, round squash. It has a dark green rind with silvery gray lines. The flesh is dark yellow-orange and tastes sweet and nutty.

Butternut squash is shaped like a large pear. It has cream-colored skin, deep orange flesh, and a sweet flavor.

Crookneck squash is a bush variety of squash that does not vine. It gets its name from its crooked shape. It has a yellow, warty rind and pale yellow flesh. It has a sweet, nutty flavor and can be eaten cooked or raw.

Hubbard squash can be dark green, grey-blue, or orange-red. The flavor is less sweet than many other kinds of squash.

Kabocha squash is a Japanese squash. It has deep green skin and orange flesh. It is sweet in flavor.

Spaghetti squash is oblong in shape. It can be cream, yellow, or orange in color. The flesh is bright yellow or orange, with many large seeds in the center. When cooked, the flesh comes out in long strands like spaghetti noodles.

Turban squash is green and either speckled or striped. It has orange-yellow flesh. It tastes a little like hazelnuts.

Zucchini squash has a green or light green skin. The almost white flesh has a light, delicate flavor. Many people think the smaller the zucchini the better the taste. It may be eaten raw or cooked, shredded in salads.

Name

All Kinds of Squash *(cont.)*

Directions: Find the different kinds of squash in the wordsearch.

B	A	M	A	O	L	C	S	Q	D	J	Z
I	N	I	H	C	C	U	Z	E	T	R	F
F	A	N	S	U	G	R	H	U	H	N	P
I	N	T	A	J	B	K	R	K	U	B	I
Y	A	L	O	V	M	B	G	N	A	L	D
O	B	E	Q	T	A	U	A	C	P	T	E
A	Q	H	B	N	R	T	G	R	O	G	L
S	K	W	I	T	A	T	F	O	D	N	Y
V	A	L	T	M	U	E	D	O	W	E	I
R	B	X	T	B	E	R	B	K	F	S	A
L	O	R	E	I	C	N	Y	N	M	O	C
C	C	Z	H	A	N	U	R	E	B	H	S
S	H	D	G	E	R	T	A	C	Q	K	N
F	A	P	A	G	O	S	N	K	H	C	W
I	D	T	P	U	C	R	E	T	T	U	B
C	R	L	S	J	A	G	O	K	C	Q	M

Word Box	
acorn	Hubbard
banana	Kabocha
buttercup	spaghetti
butternut	turban
crookneck	zucchini

Challenge: Choose a squash and find a recipe to cook it. Combine the recipes to create a class book.

Name

Leafy Greens and Dark Green Vegetables

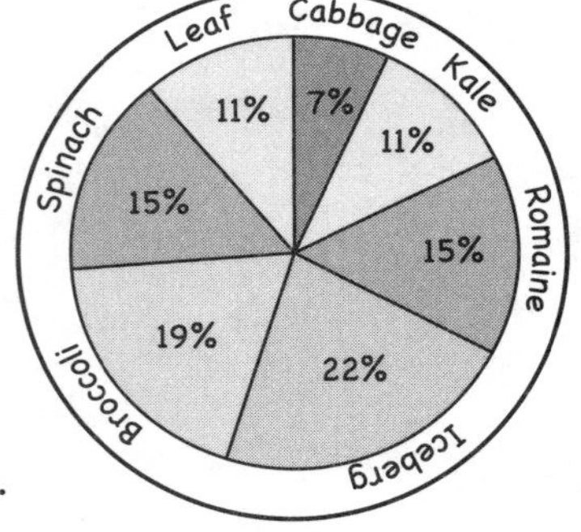

Dark green and leafy green vegetables have many nutrients, and they are low in calories. The darker the green, the healthier the vegetable! The leafy greens listed on the chart below are ranked in order from the most nutritious (1) to the least nutritious (10).

Mr. Parker's class took a survey to find out which green vegetables were their favorites. The pie graph on the right shows the results of the survey.

1. Which type of leafy green did the most students like? ______________________
2. Where does that leafy green fall on the nutrition chart below? ______________________
3. What does that number tell you?______________________
4. What percentage of students like the leafy green that is the most nutritious? ______________________
5. What is one observation you can make from this pie chart? Answer on the back of this page.

Vegetable	Description	Nutrients
1—Kale	ruffle-edged green or purple leaves	Vitamins A, C, K, calcium, folate, potassium
2—Collard Greens	smooth, dark green leaves; hearty, chewy, cabbage-like taste	Vitamins A, C, K, calcium, folate, potassium
3—Turnip Greens	smooth, dark green leaves; peppery taste	Vitamins A, C, K, calcium
4—Swiss Chard	greenish purple leaves; beet-like taste	Vitamins A, C
5—Spinach	smooth leaves; eaten raw or cooked	Vitamins A, C, folate
6—Mustard Greens	scalloped edges; peppery taste	Vitamins A, C, K, calcium
7—Broccoli	flowers and stems eaten raw or cooked	Vitamins A, C, folate, potassium
8—Romaine and Leaf Lettuce	the darker the green leaves, the more nutritious	Vitamin A, folate
9—Cabbage	red and green varieties; eaten raw or cooked	Vitamin C
10—Iceberg Lettuce	crunchy light green leaves	mostly water

Challenge: Take a vote to find your classmates' favorite dark or leafy green vegetables. Evaluate the data. Discuss ways that you might eat healthier green vegetables.

Name

Growing Vegetables in Small Places

Our fruits and vegetables come from different places. Some are grown on local or regional farms. Some are grown where the climate is right for that type of plant. Some foods, such as bananas, grow best in a tropical climate. They are shipped in from other countries.

As less farmland is available due to urban development, the agriculture industry develops new ways of growing food. We can grow certain foods at home or at school, too, using different methods. Here are two you might try:

Hydroponic Gardens: You may have heard of *hydroponic* tomatoes. Hydroponic tomatoes are grown without soil! The plants receive all the nutrients they need through their water supply. This method of growing crops for food works well because plants receive the nutrients they need to grow. Not all hydroponic systems suspend plants in water. Sometimes, sand, gravel, or coconut fibers are used to support the plants as they grow. This allows farmers to grow crops in places with limited land or soil. Plants can be grown in greenhouses, on rooftops, or even in classrooms!

Container Gardens: As more people live on the planet, being able to grow food in smaller spaces becomes more important. People can also use hydroponic principles to grow food in containers. You may know someone who has a container garden. This is a way of growing food in a very small space.

1. Find out more about vegetables that can be grown in small spaces such as a back yard garden or containers. Here are some interesting vegetables you might want to research:

   - beets
   - bush green beans
   - cabbage
   - dinosaur gourds
   - lettuce and salad greens
   - neon Swiss chard
   - peas and sweet peas
   - peppers
   - radish
   - sunflowers
   - sweet pea currant tomatoes
   - walking stick kale

2. Plan a garden. Illustrate your garden plan on the "My Garden Design" page in your journal. Add planning notes as needed. Think about the following and use your imagination:

—Will it be hydroponic or a more traditional container garden? ____________________

—What kind of vegetables would you like to grow? ____________________

____

—How many containers would you need? ____________________

—What medium would you use for your plants (e.g., sand, gravel, perlite, or just water)? ____________

____

—How would you make sure your plants got the nutrients they need? ____________________

____

—Other considerations: ____________________

Name

Think About Grains

The grains group includes foods made from wheat, rice, barley, oats, or corn. These "cereal" grains are used to make various foods, such as tortillas, pasta, and bread. Whole grains have a lot to offer:

- Grains are high in B vitamins. B vitamins help us get energy from the protein, fat, and carbohydrates in the foods we eat. They also keep our nervous system healthy.
- The magnesium found in grains helps build strong bones.
- Fiber in grains helps us digest our food.
- Folate in grains keeps our cardiovascular system healthy. It helps us make red blood cells.
- Grains have iron, which carries oxygen in the blood to the cells in our bodies.

Directions: Read this list of grains. Then, review the foods made with grains. Check the boxes of the grain foods you've eaten. Draw a star next to foods you would like to try.

Whole Grains		
☐ amaranth	☐ corn	☐ rye
☐ barley	☐ millet	☐ sorghum
☐ brown rice	☐ oats	☐ wheat
☐ buckwheat	☐ popcorn	☐ wild rice

Grain Foods		
☐ brown rice	☐ oatmeal	☐ white rice
☐ bulger (cracked wheat)	☐ oatmeal cookies	☐ whole grain cereal
☐ cornbread	☐ pitas	☐ whole grain crackers
☐ cornmeal	☐ popcorn	☐ whole wheat
☐ couscous	☐ pretzels	☐ whole wheat berries
☐ cracked wheat	☐ puffed rice cereal	☐ whole wheat bread
☐ crackers	☐ quinoa	☐ whole wheat crackers
☐ enriched white bread	☐ rolled oats	☐ whole wheat pasta
☐ flour tortillas	☐ rolls	☐ whole wheat tortillas
☐ muesli	☐ stone ground whole wheat flour	☐ wild rice
☐ noodles		

Challenge: Choose a grain or grain food you have never eaten. Find out more about it and describe how you might eat it. Add your information to your "New Healthy Foods" journal page (page 82).

Name

Corn

Corn is one of the major crops grown in the United States. People eat it fresh as a vegetable. Dried corn, including popcorn, is also considered a grain. As early as 600 AD, corn was cultivated from a wild grain known as maize grown in Central and South America. Corn is high in Vitamin A and also provides B vitamins. It is gluten-free, which makes it a good option for people who follow a gluten-free diet. Corn can be eaten with beans to provide a complete protein.

Directions: Read the clues to learn ways people eat corn as a grain in different areas of the country. Unscramble the words to find the names of these regional dishes. The first letter is highlighted for you.

1. ______________________ is a pudding-like cornbread eaten in the south.

   o e r a p o d s n b

2. ______________________ are white cornmeal pancakes from the east coast.

   a n h e j o y c n k s

3. ______________________ is corn that has been soaked in a solution of salt, soda, or lime. The soaked kernels have the germ and bran removed, leaving a soft, chewy kernel. It can be heated or put it in soup.

   n i h y o m

4. ______________________ are ground hominy. People boil them and serve them with butter or syrup for breakfast. They are also fried as cakes. This dish is most known in the South.

   s r i t g

5. ______________________ is a coarse type of corn meal made from flint corn. It is boiled to make porridge. It can also be baked in an oven or grilled. It can be used as a base for other foods such as chicken or fish.

   n o t a p l e

6. ______________________ is a type of flint corn. It has a hard hull with a pocket of starch that pops. Steam builds up inside the hull when the corn is heated, and it explodes.

   r o n p o c p

7. ______________________ is ground dried corn. It contains the bran and germ, so it is a whole grain. We use it to make cornbread, muffins, or hot cereal. Sometimes people use it to coat fish or other foods before frying or baking.

   l o m a c r e n

8. ______________________ are cornmeal batter deep fried or baked in balls with seasonings. This dish is from Native American culture in the southern United States.

   s u p e p h i s h u p

Name

Whole Grains

The two main groups of grains are whole grains and refined grains. It is recommended that half the grains we eat be whole grains. This helps us get all the nutrients we need.

- ***Whole grains*** contain all three parts of the grain kernel: the *bran,* the *germ,* and the *endosperm.*
- ***Refined grains*** have been milled (ground) to remove the bran and the germ. Refined grains have a finer texture and a longer shelf life. However, important nutrients are removed in the milling process.

"Images courtesy of Oldways and the Whole Grains Council"

There is also a third category, called "enriched" foods. ***Enriched foods*** have some of the nutrients added back in. It's better, though, to get the nutrients from a whole grain food that is not processed as much.

How can you tell if a product is made with whole grains or refined grains? You can tell by looking at the package. Either it has one of two "stamps" on it from the Whole Grains Council, or you can check the ingredients listed on the package. First, look for a stamp like the ones to the left. To get a better idea of how the stamps look on the package, fill in the stamps with a yellow highlighter.

The top stamp says 100% It means that the product is 100% whole grain. Each serving has *at least* 16 grams.

The bottom stamp, which says "Look for Whole Grain" does not have 100% on it. These products have *at least* 8 grams per serving, or half a serving of your daily grains.

If you don't see either stamp, check the ingredients. Try to find ones with the word "whole" before the grain in the ingredients. (e.g., Ingredients: whole wheat flour, instead of Ingredients: wheat flour, etc.)

Directions: Use the tips and definitions above to help you determine which of the foods on the list are whole grain foods and which are made with refined grains. Write a **W** in front of each whole grain and an **R** in front of each refined grain. You may need to do some research.

__________ **1.** 100% stone ground wheat bread

__________ **2.** animal cookies

__________ **3.** brown rice

__________ **4.** egg noodles

__________ **5.** flour tortillas

__________ **6.** oatmeal

__________ **7.** popcorn

__________ **8.** puffed rice cereal

__________ **9.** sandwich rolls

__________ **10.** whole wheat crackers

__________ **11.** whole wheat pasta

Challenge: Look at food labels and containers to find foods that are 100% whole grain, part whole grain, and "enriched." Create a class poster or display for each type to help recognize the different foods that are complete servings and those that are incomplete servings.

Name

What Does Gluten-Free Mean?

You may know someone whose diet is "gluten-free." *Gluten* is a protein found in grains, such as wheat, barley, and rye. What does it mean to have a gluten-free diet? It means you do not eat foods with gluten.

Most people who try to avoid gluten do so for health reasons. Some people have celiac disease. For these people, gluten causes inflammation in their small intestines which makes them sick. Other people have gluten intolerance and may have different symptoms. People with celiac disease or gluten intolerance should follow a gluten-free diet. This is not as easy as it might seem—gluten is everywhere! People who cannot have gluten must carefully read nutrition labels since many food products have wheat in some form. It's tricky to avoid foods containing wheat and barley. Wheat goes by many different names on food ingredient lists—*bulgur, durum flour, farina, graham flour, semolina*, and *spelt*. People who have a gluten-free diet should avoid foods with those wheat names on labels.

It is also important to read restaurant menus carefully. People who follow a gluten-free diet may have to ask questions about restaurant items or avoid certain foods. Fortunately, there are many gluten-free foods available in stores now. It is also possible to buy gluten-free flours to use in recipes for bread and other baked items. A few of the gluten-free flours include *amaranth*, *buckwheat*, *corn*, *rice*, *sorghum*, and *tapioca*.

Fruits and vegetables are gluten-free foods. Many dairy products, too, are naturally gluten-free. Protein foods such as meats are gluten-free. The trick is to make sure these meats are not breaded or marinated when they are cooked since breading and marinades are often not gluten-free.

Class Challenge

1. Spend a few days collecting packaging and advertisements for different foods.
2. Sort the foods into two groups—those that *have gluten* and those that are *gluten-free*. Pay special attention to ingredient lists to spot the different names for wheat. Circle them.
3. Create a class list of snack ideas that are gluten-free based on your findings.

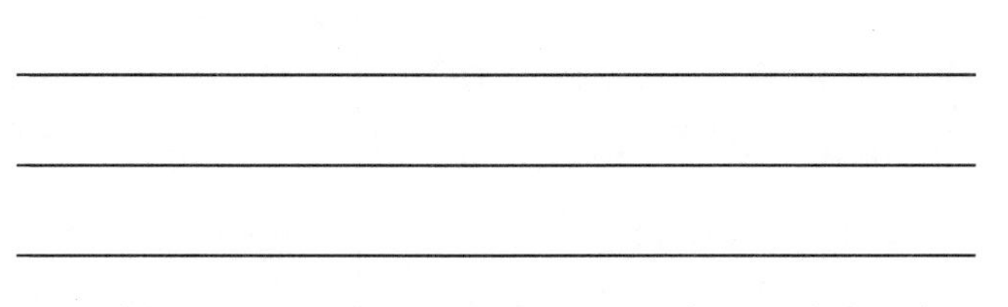

4. Consider having a special, gluten-free celebration in your classroom. What might you bring to share?

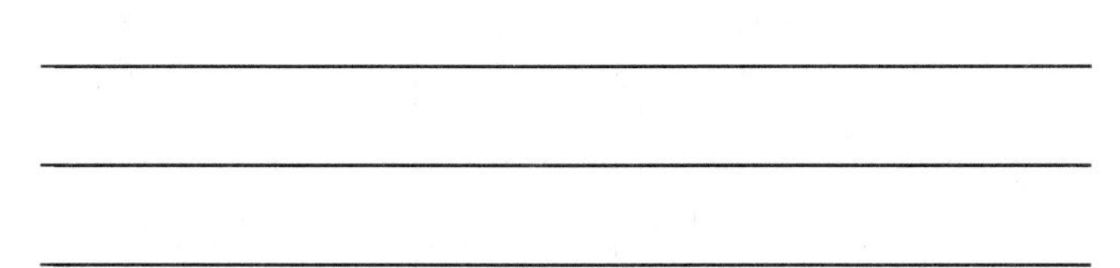

Name

Whole Grains–Spotlight on Sorghum

Directions: Use the words in the word box and other class resources to help you fill in the blanks as you read to learn more about sorghum, a whole grain.

Word Box				
	brooms	edible	Middle East	sorghum
	corn	gluten	popcorn	water
	drought	kernels	porridge	wheat

Sorghum is an important world-wide grain crop. Sorghum is a whole grain with an ____________________ hull so we get all the nutrients. This ancient cereal grain is resistant to ____________________. For this reason, it is sometimes called the "camel of crops." It was grown thousands of years ago in Egypt and spread to all of Africa and then India. Today ____________________ is grown in many countries around the world. In the United States, it is planted in the Midwest from South Dakota to Texas. The crop makes efficient use of sun and ____________________. Most ____________________ are red, white, bronze, or brown, but they can be other colors.

Like ____________________, it can be used for food, animal feed, and fuel. In some countries, it is mostly used for food. Now more people in the United States are using sorghum for food because it is ____________________ -free. People use sorghum in place of ____________________ flour in many traditional foods, such as pancakes, bread, muffins, and other baked goods. Countries around the world use sorghum in a variety of ways. In the ____________________ ____________________, sorghum is used to make couscous and flatbread. People in Honduras use it to make tortillas. African countries make sorghum into ____________________ and flatbread.

Surprise your friends with these fun facts about sorghum! A variety of sorghum called broomcorn was introduced in the United States by Benjamin Franklin. What do you think it was used for? Making ____________________! People in Africa dye some leathers red with red sorghum kernels. And finally, you can pop sorghum like____________________.

Find out something else about sorghum, and write your sorghum fact here: ____________________

____

____

____

Name

Think About Dairy Foods

The dairy group includes foods made from milk. These foods include milk, cheese, cottage cheese, yogurt, pudding, and ice cream. Dairy foods are high in calcium. Dairy foods also provide us with vitamin D, protein, and potassium. Vitamin D helps our bodies use calcium, which helps to build strong bones and teeth. Potassium helps your heart beat correctly.

Directions: Read this list of dairy foods. Check the boxes of the dairy foods you like to eat. Circle the foods you have not tried yet.

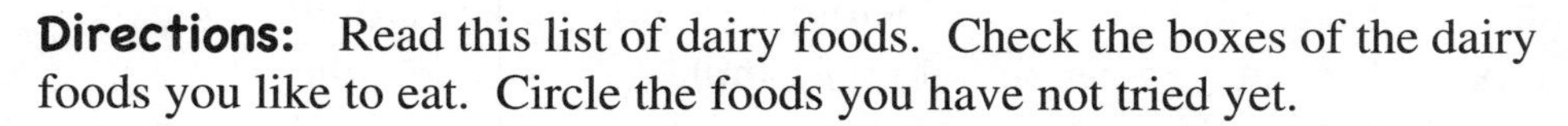

Dairy Foods

- ☐ buttermilk
- ☐ cheddar cheese
- ☐ condensed milk
- ☐ cottage cheese
- ☐ dried or powdered milk
- ☐ evaporated milk
- ☐ frozen yogurt
- ☐ Greek yogurt
- ☐ ice cream
- ☐ milk
- ☐ mozzarella cheese
- ☐ parmesan cheese
- ☐ pudding
- ☐ ricotta cheese
- ☐ swiss cheese

Note: Butter and cream cheese are not part of the dairy group because they do not retain calcium.

Challenge: Learn more about two dairy foods. Write two facts about each of these dairy foods. Then, explain why eating or drinking these foods might be a healthy addition to your diet. Add information from one of these dairy foods to your "New Healthy Foods" journal page (page 82).

Dairy Food 1 ______________________________

Fact 1 ______________________________

Fact 2 ______________________________

This food would be a healthy addition to my diet because ______________________________

____

Dairy Food 2 ______________________________

Fact 1 ______________________________

Fact 2 ______________________________

This food would be a healthy addition to my diet because ______________________________

____

Name

Types of Milk

Milk is a basic dairy food, right? Then why are there so many choices in the grocery store—and how do you choose the right one for your health needs?

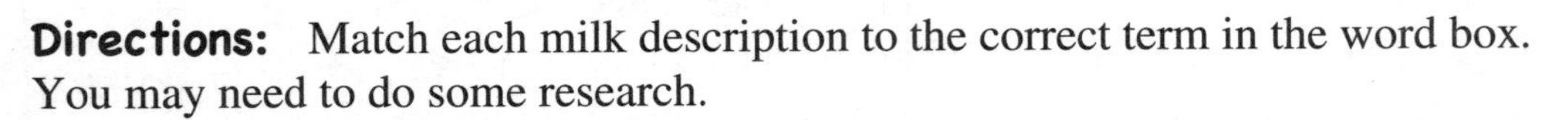

Directions: Match each milk description to the correct term in the word box. You may need to do some research.

Word Box			
buttermilk	fortified milk	lactose-free milk	reduced-fat milk
fat-free milk	homogenization	low-fat milk	whole milk
flavored milk	lactose	pasteurization	

1. Low-fat milk cultured with lactic acid bacteria. It is low in calories, with a tangy flavor.

   ____

2. A process of heating milk to destroy harmful micro-organisms, which gives milk a longer shelf life.

   ____

3. Contains 2% milk fat. It is fortified and has 10 grams of protein. ______________________________
4. This natural sugar is found in milk. ______________________________
5. This process prevents milk fat from separating from fluid milk and gives milk a smooth texture.

   ____

6. This product contains 3.5% milk fat—the amount from a cow before processing.

   ____

7. This product is treated with lactase to break down the milk sugar for people who can't digest lactose.

   ____

8. This product contains 0.2% milk fat; also called non-fat or skim. It supplies all the nutrients of whole milk. ______________________________
9. This product has sugar added but retains the nutrients in regular milk. ______________________________
10. This type of milk has the nutrients lost in processing replaced or added. For example, vitamin D is added to help bodies absorb calcium. ______________________________
11. This product contains 1% milk fat. It is rich in vitamins and minerals. ______________________________

Did you notice that the milk products contain different amounts of fat? Some fat is good for us. Our bodies need a certain amount of fat to be healthy. The question is—how much fat? For many of us, it is important to eat foods that are lower in fat, and drinking low-fat milk is a good option. For others, whole milk with more fat is important to maintain a healthy body. Each of us is different, and our ages, body types, and levels of activity all help us decide which type of milk is best for us.

Challenge: Using the information you learned from the activity, which type of milk might be the best choice for you? ______________________________

Why? ______________________________

Name

Not All Milk Comes from Cows

Many people around the world drink milk that does not come from dairy cows. Their milk comes from other animals or plants. Some people in the United States do not drink cows' milk for health reasons or as a personal preference.

1. Look at each plant or animal below. Each is a source of milk. Work in pairs or small groups to research each type of milk.
2. Write a nutrition fact about each source of milk.
3. Gather as a class and share your findings to complete the activity.
4. Use the circles to rank the different types of milk in the order you think you would try them.

(1) = most likely to try (10) = least likely to try

Alternate Sources of Milk

○ **Almond Milk**
Fact: ______________________________

○ **Camel Milk**
Fact: ______________________________

○ **Coconut Milk**
Fact: ______________________________

○ **Goat Milk**
Fact: ______________________________

○ **Hazelnuts Milk**
Fact: ______________________________

○ **Water Buffalo Milk**
Fact: ______________________________

○ **Llama Milk**
Fact: ______________________________

○ **Rice Milk**
Fact: ______________________________

○ **Sheep Milk**
Fact: ______________________________

○ **Soybean Milk**
Fact: ______________________________

Challenge: Work with classmates to create two information posters, one for plant-based milks and one for animal-based milks. Add the information you have gathered and pictures, illustrations, or product packaging to the posters.

Name

Say Cheese!

Data from the United States Department of Agriculture (USDA) indicates that we eat over 25 pounds of cheese per year per person. That's a lot of cheese! There are many different kinds of cheese, from hard cheeses to semi-soft low-fat cheeses to very soft, almost liquid cheese. We each have our favorites.

Directions: Read the clues to match the names of the cheeses to their descriptions.

1. This common yellow cheese is a hard cheese. It originated in England. It can be mild or sharp, depending on how long it is aged. ______________________________
2. This hard cheese originally came from Italy. It is made of cow's milk and has a crumbly texture. You may see it served on a sandwich. ______________________________
3. This semi-hard cheese may be made from cow, goat, or sheep's milk. It has a dense springy texture and was first made in the Netherlands. ______________________________
4. This crumbly soft cheese is used in salads. It is a popular cheese in Greece. ______________
5. This mild, creamy cheese does not have a rind. It is semi-soft, pale yellow, and made from cow's milk. It was first made in Denmark. ______________________________
6. Its name gives its origin away. First made in the region of Monterey, California, this mild cheese melts well. It is made from cow's milk and is used in Mexican cooking. ______________
7. This semi-hard cheese comes from Italy. It is made from cow's milk and has a firm, grainy texture. ______________________________
8. This soft, creamy cheese has a mild flavor. It is made from cheese curds. It may have first been made in cottages in the United States or the United Kingdom from the milk product leftover after making butter. ______________________________
9. This hard, grainy cheese from Italy has a brittle crumbly texture. It's dense and flaky and people grate it on salads, soups, or pasta, just like Parmigiano cheese. It may be made from cow's, goat's, or sheep's milk. ______________________________

Types of Cheese						
	Asiago		Feta		Monterey Jack	
	Cheddar Cheese		Gouda		Provolone	
	Cottage Cheese		Havarti		Romano	

Challenge: Find out more about cheese. You might be surprised to find out how it is made! Divide into groups to answer each of the questions. Share your findings.

Group 1—What are "curds and whey," and how do they relate to cheese?

Group 2—What does it mean when a cheese is "aged" before it is sold?

Group 3—What is American cheese?

Name

Fun with Dairy Facts

Directions: Doing research to learn more about dairy foods can help us make healthier food choices. Answer the following questions to learn more about dairy products.

1. Which states produce most of the milk in the United States? ______________________

2. Why is calcium an important nutrient? ______________________

3. Which nutrients do we get from milk? ______________________

4. Which nutrients do we get from cheese? ______________________

5. Why is yogurt good for us? ______________________

6. What is the difference between Greek yogurt and regular yogurt? ______________________

7. Why do we pasteurize milk? ______________________

8. How long does milk stay fresh in the refrigerator? ______________________

9. How much dairy should you have each day? ______________________

10. What is the difference between whole milk and low-fat milk? ______________________

11. Which dairy product is a treat or "sometimes" food? ______________________

    Why? ______________________

Challenge: Create a set of Dairy Fact Question Cards to share what you learned.

1. Write one question on each card. Put the answer to the question on the back.
2. Make your cards as interesting as possible to encourage others to learn and make healthy choices about dairy, too. Add pictures and drawings.
3. Quiz each other.

Name

Think About Protein Foods

We get protein from different kinds of meat, such as beef, chicken, and other animals. Seafood is another good source of protein. We can also get protein from legumes, beans and peas, eggs, nuts, and seeds.

Our muscles and organs are made out of different types of tissues. Protein helps build and maintain these tissues in our bodies. Protein also helps our bodies fight disease to stay healthy. Protein-rich foods provide us with B vitamins and minerals such as iron and magnesium.

- The B vitamins help our bodies get energy from our food. They keep our nervous system and circulatory system healthy.
- Iron helps our blood vessels carry oxygen to all parts of our bodies.
- Magnesium helps build strong bones and releases energy when needed from our muscles.

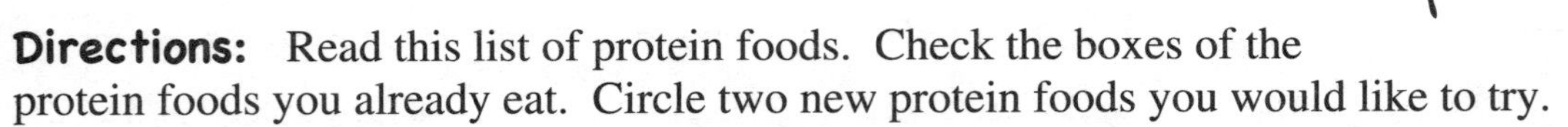

Directions: Read this list of protein foods. Check the boxes of the protein foods you already eat. Circle two new protein foods you would like to try.

Protein Foods

☐ almonds	☐ ground lamb	☐ pumpkin seeds
☐ beef	☐ ground pork	☐ rabbit
☐ bison	☐ ground turkey	☐ sesame seeds
☐ black beans	☐ ham	☐ shellfish
☐ black-eyed peas	☐ hazelnuts	☐ soybeans
☐ cashews	☐ kidney beans	☐ split peas
☐ chicken	☐ lamb	☐ sunflower seeds
☐ chickpeas	☐ lima beans	☐ tuna
☐ duck	☐ navy beans	☐ turkey
☐ eggs	☐ peanuts	☐ veal
☐ fish	☐ pecans	☐ venison
☐ goose	☐ pinto beans	☐ walnuts
☐ ground beef	☐ pistachios	
☐ ground chicken	☐ pork	

Challenge: Research a new protein food you would like to try. Discuss the nutrients found in this food and why you would like to try it. Use your "New Healthy Foods" journal page (page 82) to record your findings.

Name

Types of Protein

The protein in foods is made up of smaller molecules called amino acids. Protein has many different amino acids. Amino acids are the building blocks to every cell in our bodies. Scientists have identified 22 amino acids that help our bodies stay healthy. Our bodies make 13 of these amino acids, but we have to get the other nine from foods we eat.

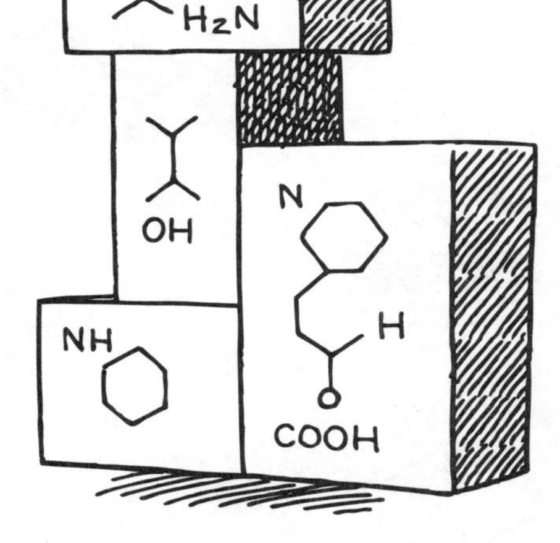

Some protein contains all the amino acids we need. This is called *complete protein*, and it is found in foods from animals, such as meat and dairy foods. Other foods with protein, such as vegetables and legumes, lack one or more of the amino acids we need. We call this type of protein an *incomplete protein*. People who do not eat animal foods can combine incomplete protein foods to make sure they get all the amino acids they need. Legumes can be paired with grains to form a source of complete protein.

Remember, we do not need to have all of the amino acids at every meal. As long as you eat a variety of foods during a day or week, your body should get everything it needs.

1. Fill in the chart with examples of each type of protein.

Complete Protein	Incomplete Protein

2. Do some research. What are some examples of foods you can combine to make a complete source of protein? The first one has been done for you.

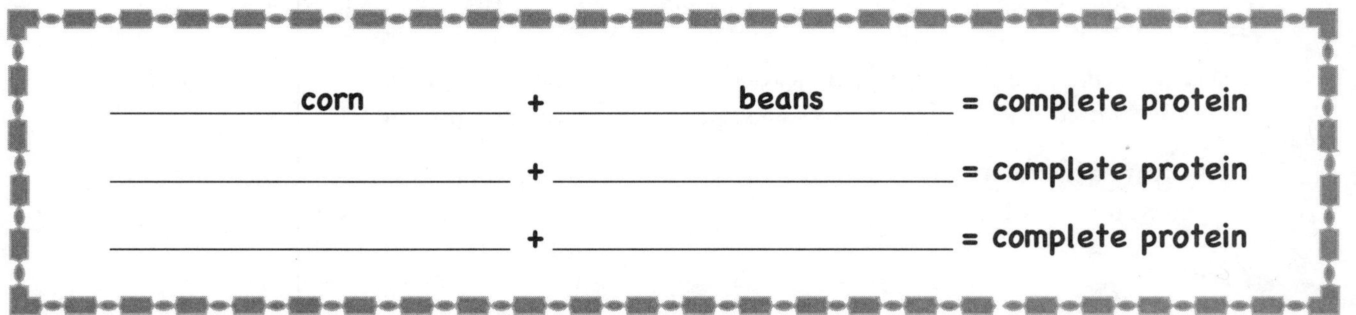

3. What are your three favorite sources of protein?

_______________ _______________ _______________

Name

Do You Know Your Food Animals?

Around the world, people eat meat from different animals. In the United States, we often think of beef, which comes from cattle, when we think of meat. We also eat pork, which is meat that comes from pigs. Some people prefer mutton, or meat from sheep. Chickens also supply us with meat.

Directions: Draw lines to match these foods to the animal that supplies the meat. For some, you may have more than one possibility. Color the foods you eat and the animal that each one comes from.

Directions: Fill in the blanks with the meat or the animal it comes from to solve these riddles.

1. Have you ever had a BLT? It is a sandwich made with strips of meat called ____________________.

The strips of meat come from a ____________________.

It is topped with lettuce and tomato.

2. I am a patty served on a round bun. Lettuce, tomatoes, and cheese are added.

Sometimes I am eaten with french fries.

I am a ____________________.

I come from a grazing animal called a ____________________.

3. My meat is ground for a breakfast food that is shaped into patties or links.

My patties or links can be served with eggs or on a hot biscuit.

I am a ____________________.

4. A steak is one of many cuts of meat you can get from me.

Some ranchers raise a breed called Angus which is very good for steaks.

I am a ____________________.

Challenge: Chicken is one type of poultry that is good source of protein. How many other types of poultry that people eat can you name? Make a list on the back of this page.

Name

All Kinds of Nuts

Many people enjoy eating nuts as a snack food or in other foods, such as meat dishes, salads, and desserts. Along with protein, nuts provide us with many vitamins and nutrients.

Directions: The charts below provide the nutrient content of different types of nuts. The amounts shown are based on one-ounce servings of nuts, which may be more than a serving for some people.

	Number of nuts in 1 oz.	Calories	Fat	Sodium	Potassium	Carbohydrate	Fiber	Sugar	Protein
almond	22	163	14 g	0 mg	200 mg	6 g	3.5 g	1.1 g	6 g
brazil nut	6–8	186	19 g	1 mg	187 mg	3.5 g	2.1g	0.7 g	4.1 g
cashew	18	157	12 g	3 mg	187 mg	9 g	0.9 g	1.7 g	5 g
chestnut	3	43	0.2 g	1 mg	87 mg	10 g	1.4 g	3 g	0.8 g
hazelnut	20	178	17 g	0 mg	193 mg	4.7 g	2.7 g	1.2 g	4.2 g
macadamia	10–12	204	21 g	1 mg	104 mg	3.9 g	2.4 g	1.3 g	2.2 g
pecan	20	201	21 g	0 mg	120 mg	3.8 g	2.7 g	1.2 g	2.7 g
pine nut	167	191	19 g	1 mg	169 mg	3.7 g	1 g	1 g	3.9 g
pistachio	47	159	13 g	0 mg	291 mg	8 g	2.9 g	2.2 g	6 g
walnut	14	175	17 g	1 mg	148 mg	2.8 g	1.9 g	0.3 g	7 g

Nut	Vitamin C	Vitamin B-6	Calcium	Magnesium	Iron
almond			7%	19%	5%
brazil nut			4%	26%	3%
cashew		5%	1%	20%	10%
chestnut	11%	5%		4%	1%
hazelnut	3%	10%	3%	11%	7%
macadamia		5%	2%	9%	5%
pecan		5%	2%	9%	4%
pine nut				17%	8%
pistachio	2%	25%	3%	8%	6%
walnut		10%	1%	14%	4%

1. Which nut will taste the saltiest without adding any extra salt? ____________________
2. Nuts are a good source of which nutrients? ____________________
3. Which nuts do you like to eat? ____________________
4. Discuss your observations about different types of nuts after reading these charts.

Name

Wild About Seeds

Nuts and seeds are included in the protein group. It's easy to recognize common nuts we eat, but we don't always think about eating seeds. There are many ways to eat seeds:

- Roast seeds and eat them as a snack.
- Use seeds to season foods.
- Add seeds to baked goods or other foods to add flavor and texture.
- Sprinkle seeds on salads or other vegetables for a special treat.

Savory Seeds

 caraway
 flax
 pumpkin
dill
poppy
 sesame
sunflower

Directions: Read the clues to learn about different seeds people eat. Fill in the lines below with the correct letters for each seed name.

1. You may have had these small brown seeds in multi-grain crackers.

   ____ ____ ____ ____

2. People often add these tiny black seeds to muffins and bagels.

   ____ ____ ____ ____ ____

3. These savory seeds are related to parsley. They look like small dark grains of rice and are used in rye bread and curry dishes.

   ____ ____ ____ ____ ____ ____ ____

4. You may have seen these tear-drop-shaped white seeds on your hamburger buns or on a bagel.

   ____ ____ ____ ____ ____ ____

5. These seeds have striped or black shells, and are named after a flower. We eat them salted as a snack or on salads.

   ____ ____ ____ ____ ____ ____ ____ ____ ____

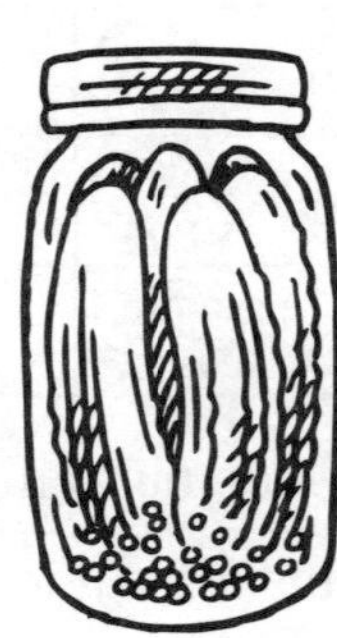

6. You may associate this seasoning or seed with a type of pickles, but it can also be used in place of caraway in breads, or mixed with a bit of butter to make a savory spread for bread.

   ____ ____ ____ ____

7. People roast these squash seeds in the fall, especially in October.

   ____ ____ ____ ____ ____ ____ ____

Name

Fish and Shellfish Crossword

Fish and shellfish (crustaceans) are part of the protein food group. These important foods provide us with omega-3 fatty acids, which are healthy kinds of fat. Eating fish helps lower cholesterol. Some scientists think they also reduce certain inflammations in our bodies. Fish also provides vitamin D, which helps our bodies absorb calcium and build strong bones.

Directions: Use the clues on the following page to fill in this crossword puzzle.

Word Box			
	clams	lobster	shrimp
	cod	perch	tilapia
	crab	salmon	trout
	halibut	scallops	tuna

Note: Fish prepared in healthy ways, such as baking or broiling, is recommended.

Name

Fish and Shellfish Crossword *(cont.)*

Directions: Use the clues below to fill in the crossword on page 47.

Across

2.	This type of fish is born in fresh water. Then, it migrates to the ocean where it spends its adult life. Later, it returns to the freshwater stream to spawn.
3.	This chunky fish has a humped back. Some species live in the ocean and some live in fresh water.
5.	This flaky white fish is a good source of phosphorus, niacin, and vitamin B-12. It lives on the ocean floor.
7.	This shellfish is related to clams, mussels, and oysters. Unlike clams and mussels, this shellfish can swim. People eat the muscle of the animal, which is a good source of potassium and vitamin B-12.
8.	These colorful fish are native to lakes and streams in the western United States. Some adults migrate to the ocean but return to fresh water to spawn. They are a good source of calcium.
10.	People like this white fish for its mild flavor and availability, which makes it lower in price than other fish. It's a good source of potassium and vitamins B-6 and B-12.

Down

1.	Often this seafood is eaten steamed or in chowder. It is very high in vitamin B-12 and iron. It also has vitamins A and C.
2.	This popular crustacean is found worldwide in both fresh and saltwater. Like other seafood, it is a good source of protein and also of selenium. Be careful not to eat the tail!
4.	These shellfish have 10 legs. The species we are most familiar with lives off the coast of the Atlantic Ocean. They are high in cholesterol, but are a good source of protein and vitamin B-12.
6.	This deep-water fish is the largest flat fish in the ocean. The flesh has a dense, firm texture. This fish has a low fat content and is high in potassium.
8.	We often eat this saltwater finfish as part of a sandwich. Most come from California. This saltwater fish swims over 50 mph in the ocean and is always in motion.
9.	If this crustacean loses a claw, it grows back. People sometimes use the cooked meat on salads. A good source of protein, this food also provides magnesium.

Name

Legumes

Legumes are plants with seeds that grow in pods. Peas, beans, lentils, and peanuts are all legumes. These foods are in the vegetable group, but they are also in the protein group. They are a good source of protein as well as fiber and potassium. People eat legumes as vegetables or as a protein food. Many legumes make healthy snack food choices in place of other snack foods. Compare these snack foods.

Legume Snacks	"Sometimes Foods" Snacks
Peanuts *Serving = 1 oz.* Each serving has these nutrients: • 164 calories • 1 g sugar • 7 g protein • 2% of daily calcium • 2 g fiber • 4% of daily iron	**Peanut Candy Bar** *Serving = 2 oz.* This snack has: • 260 calories • 30 g sugar • 5 g protein • 2% of daily calcium • 2 g fiber • 4% of daily iron
Hummus Dip *Serving = 1 tbsp* This dip is made with chickpeas, also called garbanzo beans. • 25 calories • 34 mg potassium • 1.2 g protein	**Ranch Dip** *Serving = 1 tbsp* People eat this dip with vegetables, chips, or crackers. It may include dairy ingredients. • 30 calories • 0 mg potassium • .5 g protein
Baked Lentil Chips *4.5 oz. bag of chips = 4.5 servings* Each 1 oz. serving has: • 110 calories • 2.5 g fat • 3 g fiber • 4 g protein • 6% iron • 6% calcium • 0% vitamin C • 0% vitamin B6	**Potato Chips** *1 oz. serving (15 chips)* This snack has: • 150 calories • 10 g fat • 1 g fiber • 2 g protein • 10% vitamin C • 10% vitamin B6 • 0% iron • 0% calcium

1. Compare the similar snacks in each row. What are some reasons legume snacks make healthier snack choices than the "sometimes foods" snacks? ______________________________

   ____

2. What is one legume snack you would like to try? ______________________________

   Why? ______________________________

3. What are the pros and cons of your food choice? Use a blank journal page to explain.

Name

Local Foods

Do you know which foods are grown in your local area or state? Some parts of the United States are known for growing certain fruits or vegetables. For example, when you think of oranges, you think of Florida or California. Vegetables such as okra, eggplant, and collard or mustard greens are associated with the Southern states.

okra

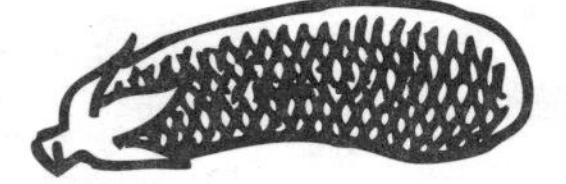
eggplant

collard or mustard greens

Although fruit is grown across the United States, some areas produce larger amounts of certain fruits to sell. For instance, many apples sold in stores come from Washington or Michigan. Michigan is the largest producer of blueberries. Peaches come from California, Georgia, and South Carolina.

apple

blueberries

peach

Where do vegetables come from? The states that grow the most asparagus are California, Washington, and Michigan. California and Florida are leading producers of tomatoes. Fresh corn has a relatively short season in stores. The rest of the year many people buy and eat canned or frozen corn. This processed corn comes from Wisconsin and Minnesota.

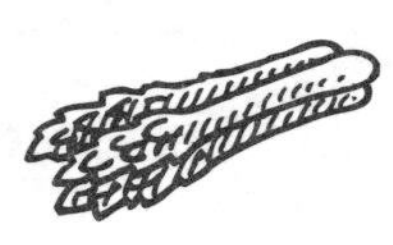
asparagus

tomato

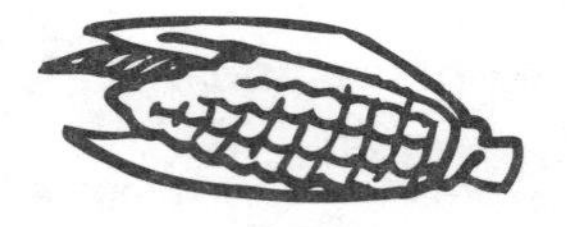
corn

Research to learn more about healthy foods that are grown in your area.

1. List a fruit and a vegetable you enjoy eating. Find out if they are grown locally or if they are transported to your local stores.

Fruit: ____________________________ **is grown in** ____________________________________.

Vegetable: ____________________________ **is grown in** ________________________________.

2. Why is it a good idea to eat foods that are grown in your state or region?

____

____

3. What would be good about having foods that come from other places?

____

____

Challenge: On the "Local Foods" page in your journal (page 85), draw a map of your state. Add pictures or illustrations of the major fruit and vegetable crops in your state based on your research.

Name

Organic Foods

Some labels in the grocery store state that foods are "organic." That means they are foods that are grown, raised, or processed using different methods:

- Farmers rotate organic crops to enhance soil nutrition. They try to conserve soil and water and reduce pollution.
- Farmers use natural predators or barriers to protect organic crops from pests. They don't use chemicals to fertilize or control weeds.
- Ranchers raise animals without using chemicals to reduce disease. They make sure the animals get fresh air. The animals eat organic foods that are not treated with pesticides. Ranchers keep the animals as healthy as possible by giving them balanced diets and clean living conditions.

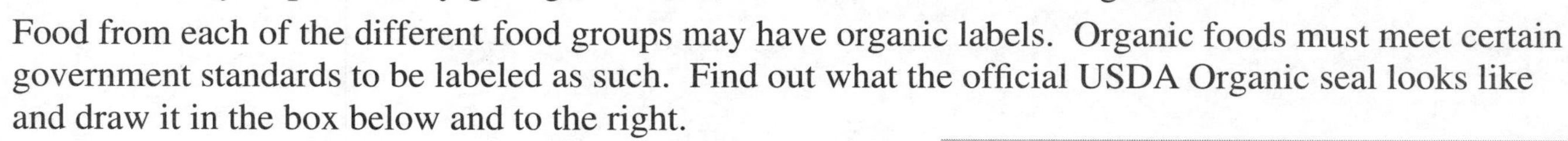

Food from each of the different food groups may have organic labels. Organic foods must meet certain government standards to be labeled as such. Find out what the official USDA Organic seal looks like and draw it in the box below and to the right.

- 100% Organic foods are single ingredient foods like a fruit, vegetable, milk, meat, or cheese that have been grown following specific guidelines. Often these foods wear a USDA Organic seal.
- An "organic" food product with more than one ingredient must be ninety-five percent organic to wear the "USDA Organic" seal.
- Products that are more than 70% organic can be labeled "organic" but cannot have the seal.

Why eat organic foods?

Some people choose organic foods because they are concerned that residue from pesticides may remain on the food. People also eat organic foods because they do not want preservatives added to their food. Another reason to choose organic foods is out of concern for the environment. Organic farming methods do not use chemicals. Organic growers want to make the best possible use of natural resources.

Organic foods tend to cost more because farming practices are more expensive. These foods may not look quite as perfect in size or shape or color, but they meet the same government standards for safety and nutritional value.

1. What makes something an "organic" food? ____________________
2. How can you tell if a food is organic? ____________________
3. What is a preservative? ____________________
4. Why might someone want to eat organic foods? ____________________
5. What kinds of foods can be labeled organic? ____________________
6. How do organic foods help the environment? ____________________

Challenge: The words *natural* and *organic* on a label do not mean the same thing. What is a natural food? ____________________

Directions: Use this chart to complete page 53.

What's in Your Food?

Read the Nutrition Label

The serving size tells you what is a reasonable portion. The nutrition facts listed on this label represent the nutrition in one serving.

This section shows total fat and types of fat, cholesterol, and sodium. While oils and fats are part of a healthy diet, too many of the items in this section can be unhealthy.

The carbohydrates and protein are listed here. Foods low in sugar and high in fiber—two types of carbohydrates—are usually a healthy choice. Protein is an important part of good nutrition as well.

In this section, you can see what vitamins and minerals are in the food. It shows the percentage of daily value in one serving of the food.

Nutrition Facts

Serving Size 1 slice (48g)
Servings Per Container 6

Amount Per Serving

Calories 252 **Calories From Fat** 108

	% Daily Value*
Total Fat 12g	18%
Saturated Fat 3g	15%
Trans Fat	
Cholesterol 30mg	10%
Sodium 480mg	20%
Total Carbohydrate 28g	9%
Dietary Fiber 3g	12%
Sugars 5g	
Protein 8g	
Vitamin A	4%
Vitamin C	8%
Calcium	20%
Iron	4%

*Percent Daily Values are based on a 2,000 calorie diet. Your daily values may be higher or lower depending on your calorie needs:

	Calories	2,000	2,500
Total Fat	Less than	65g	80g
Saturated Fat	Less than	20g	25g
Cholesterol	Less than	300mg	300mg
Sodium	Less than	2,400mg	2,400mg
Total Carbohydrate		300g	375g
Dietary Fiber		25g	30g

The calorie information shows you how many total calories are in each serving, and how many of the calories are from fat.

This column shows the recommended amount of each nutrient contained in a serving. It serves as a guide to help people eat the things their bodies need to be healthy.

Your daily nutritional needs may be more or less than those listed on the label. Here is a summary of important nutrition guidelines for someone who eats 2,000 or 2,500 calories a day.

Name

Look at the Label!

1. Use the "What's in Your Food?" chart on page 52 to complete this chart.

Nutrition Label Information		
Serving Size		
Servings per Container		
Calories per Serving		
Fat Calories		
Per Serving	**Amount**	**% Daily Value**
Total Fat		
Saturated Fat		
Cholesterol		
Sodium		
Total Carbohydrate		
Dietary Fiber		
Sugars		
Protein		
Vitamin A		
Vitamin C		
Calcium		
Iron		

2. Why is it so important to look at the nutrition labels on foods? ______________________________

____

____

Name

What Counts as One Serving?

The nutrition information listed on the nutrition label is for the suggested serving amount, not the whole container or package. It tells us how many calories and other nutrients are in that suggested serving. One cup of pasta is two ounces, so it counts as two one-ounce equivalents of grain, or $\frac{2}{5}$ of your daily grain.

2 cups of pasta = _______ one-ounce equivalents of grain, or _______ of your daily grain.

Below are some guidelines to help you think about serving sizes. (Think of a cup of fruit as taking up the same room as a baseball.) In each food group, serving suggestions are made. Other foods in the food group can be substituted.

Directions: Use the chart to find out how many servings of each food group are suggested for students 10–12 years old to eat each day. Read the suggestions to get an idea of serving sizes, and answer the questions on the following page.

Fruit	Vegetables
Daily Amount: *$1\frac{1}{2}$ cups* 1 medium apple or orange (1 cup equivalent) 1 cup cut fruit (baseball) $\frac{1}{2}$ cup grapes ($\frac{1}{2}$ baseball) 1 serving raisins (golf ball) (1 cup equivalent)	**Daily Amount:** *2 cups* $\frac{1}{2}$ cup cut up vegetables ($\frac{1}{2}$ baseball) 1 cup vegetables (baseball) 1 medium baked potato (1 cup equivalent)

Grains	
Daily Amount: *5 one-ounce equivalents*	
1 small bagel (2 ounces—3" diameter) 1 cup cooked pasta (2 one-ounce equivalents) (baseball) 1 cup cereal (baseball) (1 oz. equivalent)	1 cup popcorn (baseball) $\frac{1}{2}$ cup rice ($\frac{1}{2}$ baseball) 1 wheat pancake/waffle (diameter of a CD) (1 oz.) 1 biscuit (2" diameter) (2 oz. equivalent)

Protein	Dairy
Daily Amount: *5 one-ounce equivalents* 1 T. peanut butter (1 oz. equivalent) $\frac{1}{4}$ cup nuts (golf ball) (1 oz. equivalent) 3 ounces meat or fish (palm of adult hand) 1 ounce meatball (1" diameter) 1 egg (1 oz. equivalent) $\frac{1}{4}$ cup cooked beans ($\frac{1}{2}$ baseball) (1 oz. equivalent) 1 ounce lunch meat (slice size of a CD) 1 small, lean hamburger (2 or 3 one-ounce equivalents)	**Daily Amount:** *3 cups* 1 oz. cheese (1 cup) (4 dice) 1 cup cottage cheese (baseball) $\frac{1}{2}$ cup hard cheese (1 slice) 1 cup milk or yogurt (baseball) $\frac{1}{2}$ cup frozen yogurt ($\frac{1}{2}$ baseball)

Challenge: Create a display using CDs, golf balls, baseballs and $\frac{1}{2}$ baseballs, etc. to show serving sizes.

Name

What Counts as One Serving? *(cont.)*

Directions: Think about what you have had to eat today or make a plan for what you will eat tomorrow. Use the chart on the previous page to help you with serving portions.

1. List the foods you have eaten today in the appropriate food group section below.

	What Foods Have You Eaten Today?	Have You Had Your Recommended Amount?
Fruits $1\frac{1}{2}$ cups/day	____________ ____________ ____________	1 c. $\frac{1}{2}$ c.
Veggies 2 cups/day	____________ ____________ ____________	1 c. 1 c.
Grains 5 oz./day	____________ ____________ ____________	1 oz. 1 oz. 1 oz. 1 oz. 1 oz.
Dairy 3 cups/day	____________ ____________ ____________	1 c. 1 c. 1 c.
Protein 5 oz./day	____________ ____________ ____________	1 oz. 1 oz. 1 oz. 1 oz. 1 oz.

2. Did you have more than one "serving" of certain foods at a time? ____________

   Which foods? ____________

3. Are there food groups you have not yet filled? ____________

   ____

4. List the "sometimes foods" you have had today: ____________

   ____________ ____________ ____________

5. Use a different colored pencil to write in foods you *might eat* to create balanced meals or snacks.

Journal Page: Now you have a better understanding of how to choose foods to eat. Try tracking your servings for a whole day. Use the "Track Your Servings" page in your journal.

Name

Calories

Eating healthy foods keeps us energized and helps our bodies function properly. The foods we eat have carbohydrates, fats, and protein, which provide energy and nutrients for our bodies. The energy we get from food is measured in the form of *calories.* We need a certain number of calories to maintain the right level of energy. However, the number of calories a person needs can vary depending on his or her age, gender, and activity level. Some people need about 1,200 calories per day. Others need over two thousand calories per day. Athletes can consume even more!

Your calories (energy from food) should be balanced:

Protein found in foods such as meat, fish, chicken, eggs, and milk should make up 10–30% of your daily intake.

Carbohydrates found in foods such as whole grains, milk, fruits, and vegetables should make up 45–65% of your daily intake.

Healthy Fats found in foods such as avocados, olives, nuts, seeds, and fish should make up 25–35% of your daily intake.

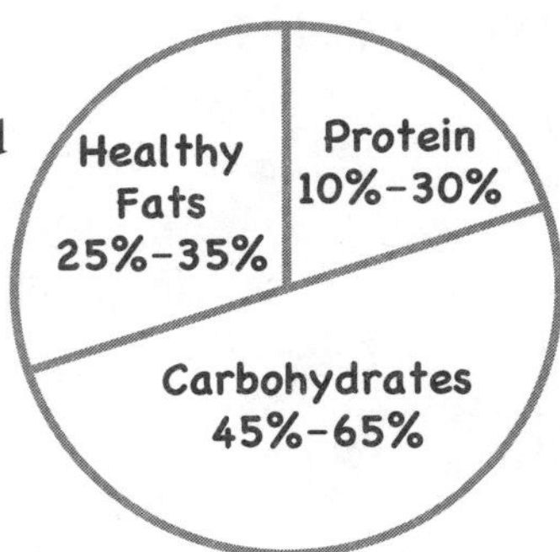

Empty Calories

Not all foods are equally nutritious for us. Some do not have enough protein, healthy fats, or carbohydrates. Junk foods have high levels of calories from sugar or fat, but do not provide much protein, vitamins, or minerals. These "empty calories" do not help us maintain healthy bodies or give us the energy we need to perform daily activities.

It is important to check the ingredients and watch portion sizes when choosing foods to eat. For instance, a hamburger could be considered a healthy food or a junk food. It depends on what kind of meat is used, how it is prepared, and what is put on it. Leaner cuts of meat tend to be healthier choices. A whole-wheat bun might have more nutrients than one made with a white bread bun. If you add lettuce and tomato to the hamburger, it will be more nutritious than if you simply add ketchup. And sweet potato fries are healthier for you than regular french fries because sweet potatoes have more nutrients than white potatoes.

It is important for your body to have a balance of healthy foods every day and to enjoy "sometimes" foods once in a while, since they have fewer nutrients but more empty calories.

What Is "Supersized"?

Another way people consume too many empty calories is by eating portion sizes that are too large. What do you think it means to "supersize" a meal? It means you will get a larger portion of food than a regular order. For example, at a fast food restaurant, you might supersize your meal to get more french fries or a larger hamburger. The bigger the meal, the more calories consumed, but we know that all calories are not the same. You may not be getting more of the nutrients you need when you supersize a meal, but you will be getting more empty calories. To maintain a healthy weight, it is best to have smaller portions unless you are very active.

Challenge: Use the "Calories" page in your journal (page 88) to share what you have learned about calories.

Name

Natural Sugar and Added Sugar

Do you know how much sugar is in the foods you eat? You can often find out by checking the nutrition label. Sometimes sugar is a natural part of a food, like the sugar in fruit. Bananas and oranges have quite a bit of natural sugar. Tomatoes and snow peas have a little natural sugar. These are still healthy foods because they have many other nutrients. Milk also has sugar in it, but it is not added sugar.

Other items, like cookies or sweetened drinks, have sugar added. The label on the right shows you where to find the amount of sugar in a food. The label to the right is for a sports drink.

The amounts of nutrients listed on labels are for one serving of that food. Sometimes people eat more than one serving of a food at a time. For example, the label for the sports drink is for two servings. If you drink the whole drink at one time, you have consumed double the amount of sugar, calories, and other nutrients listed on the label.

Sports Drink

Nutrition Facts
Serving Size 8 fl oz (240g)
Servings Per Container 2

Amount Per Serving	
Calories 70	
	%Daily Value*
Total Fat 0g	0 %
Saturated Fat 0g	0 %
Trans Fat 0g	
Cholesterol 0mg	0 %
Sodium 55mg	2 %
Total Carbohydrate 20g	7 %
Dietary Fiber 0g	0 %
Sugars 19g	
Protein 3g	
Vitamin A 0% • Vitamin C 0%	
Calcium 0% • Iron 0%	

* Percent Daily Values are based on a 2,000 calorie diet.

LOW=5% or less HIGH=20% or more

1. Circle the amount of "servings per container."
2. How much sugar will you consume if you drink the whole drink? ______ g
3. What nutrients do you get from a sports drink?

    ____

4. The chart below shows how much hidden sugar is in everyday "processed" foods. Do the math to fill in the missing spaces on the chart. Round your answers as needed to find an estimate.

1 tsp. sugar = 4g sugar

Food	Grams of Sugar per Serving	Teaspoons
barbeque sauce	13 g	
chocolate bar	27 g	
cola soda		$6\frac{3}{4}$ teaspoons (average)
graham crackers	7 g	
granola bars		2 teaspoons (average)
peanut butter	3 g	
raisin bran cereal		4 teaspoons (average)
saltine crackers		0 teaspoons
spaghetti sauce	8 g (average)	
yogurt		6 teaspoons

5. Which food surprised you most with its amount of sugar? ______________________
6. Which two foods have the same amount of sugar per serving?

    ______________________ ______________________

Name

Natural Sugar and Added Sugar *(cont.)*

It is important to eat a variety of healthy foods every day and to save treats for special times. We know that foods like cookies, candy, ice cream, and some drinks have *added* sugar. It is easy to check the nutrition labels to see how much sugar. Some health organizations say children should have no more than six or seven teaspoons of *added* sugar per day.

1. Do the math: 1 teaspoon = 4 grams 6 teaspoons equals __________ grams
2. It is suggested that children have no more than ___________ grams of added sugar per day.

Directions: Compare the nutrition labels below and circle the sugars on each label. Circle the serving sizes too. Check the amount of sugar in each. Then, answer the questions below.

2% Milk

Nutrition Facts	
Serving Size 8 fl oz (244g)	
Servings Per Container 8	
Amount Per Serving	
Calories 120 Calories from Fat 40	
	%Daily Value*
Total Fat 4.5g	7 %
Saturated Fat 3g	15 %
Trans Fat 0g	
Cholesterol 20mg	6 %
Sodium 120mg	5 %
Total Carbohydrate 12g	4 %
Dietary Fiber 0g	0 %
Sugars 11g	
Protein 8g	
Vitamin A 10% • Vitamin C 4%	
Calcium 30% • Iron 0%	
* Percent Daily Values are based on a 2,000 calorie diet.	

LOW=5% or less HIGH=20% or more

Cola Soda

Nutrition Facts	
Serving Size 8 fl oz (240g)	
Servings Per Container 1.5	
Amount Per Serving	
Calories 100	
	%Daily Value*
Total Fat 0g	0 %
Saturated Fat 0g	0 %
Trans Fat 0g	
Cholesterol 0mg	0 %
Sodium 35mg	0 %
Total Carbohydrate 27g	9 %
Dietary Fiber 0g	0 %
Sugars 27g	
Protein 0g	
Vitamin A 0% • Vitamin C 0%	
Calcium 0% • Iron 0%	
* Percent Daily Values are based on a 2,000 calorie diet.	

LOW=5% or less HIGH=20% or more

Low-Calorie Cola

Nutrition Facts	
Serving Size 8 fl oz (240g)	
Servings Per Container 1	
Amount Per Serving	
Calories 0	
	%Daily Value*
Total Fat 0g	0 %
Saturated Fat 0g	0 %
Trans Fat 0g	
Cholesterol 0mg	0 %
Sodium 30mg	1 %
Total Carbohydrate 0g	0 %
Dietary Fiber 0g	0 %
Sugars 0g	
Protein 0g	
Vitamin A 0% • Vitamin C 0%	
Calcium 0% • Iron 0%	
* Percent Daily Values are based on a 2,000 calorie diet.	

LOW=5% or less HIGH=20% or more

3. Which beverage has the most sugar? ____________________
4. Which beverage has the least sugar? ____________________
5. Compare the vitamin information on the three labels. What did you find? ____________________

   ____
6. Which of the three drinks do you think is the healthiest? ____________________

   Why? ____________________

Challenge: Check the labels to find the amounts of sugar in two foods you eat in one day. Don't forget to look at the serving size at the top of the label to compute the right amount of sugar.

Food 1 ____________________ **Amount of Sugar** ____________________

Food 2 ____________________ **Amount of Sugar** ____________________

Add the two amounts to see how much sugar you got from these two foods. _________ grams

How many teaspoons of sugar did you consume? ____________________

Extension: Fill an 8-ounce container with the amount of sugar found in a cola soda. Create a display to show the amounts of sugar in other food items.

Name

What Is Fiber?

Fiber is the part of the plant we eat that our bodies cannot break down to use for energy. Instead, fiber is useful in other ways—it helps us digest our food and it helps maintain a good blood sugar level. How much fiber do you need each day? As with most nutrients, it varies depending on health and activity, but here are some guidelines.

4–8 year-olds	25 g/day
9–13-year-old boys	31 g/day
9–13-year-old girls	26 g/day
14–18-year-old boys	38 g/day
14–18-year-old girls	26 g/day

High fiber foods provide many nutrients and are also low-calorie foods. There are two types of plant fiber:

Type 1 dissolves in water. This type of fiber helps keep our blood sugar at the right level. It can also lower cholesterol. We can find the type of fiber that dissolves in water in the following foods. Underline the ones you eat.

- whole grains, such as barley and oatmeal
- fruits, such as apples, blueberries, kiwi fruit, oranges, pears, plums, and strawberries
- protein foods, such as lentils, nuts, flaxseeds, and beans
- vegetables, such as cucumbers, celery, and carrots

Type 2 does not dissolve in water. This type of fiber helps us digest our food. Good sources of fiber that do not dissolve in water include the following foods. Underline the ones you eat.

- whole grain foods
- dark leafy vegetables, celery, broccoli, cabbage, and carrots
- raisins and grapes

Directions: Read the nutrition labels on the right. They provide important information about the foods you eat.

Beans, kidney, canned

Nutrition Facts
Serving Size 1/2 cup (128g)
Servings Per Container 4

Amount Per Serving	
Calories 110	
	%Daily Value*
Total Fat 0g	0 %
Saturated Fat 0g	0 %
Trans Fat 0g	
Cholesterol 0mg	0 %
Sodium 440mg	18 %
Total Carbohydrate 20g	7 %
Dietary Fiber 8g	33 %
Sugars 3g	
Protein 7g	
Vitamin A 0% • Vitamin C 2%	
Calcium 4% • Iron 8%	

* Percent Daily Values are based on a 2,000 calorie diet.

LOW=5% or less HIGH=20% or more

Banana

Nutrition Facts
Serving Size 1 banana (118g)
Servings Per Container 6

Amount Per Serving	
Calories 110	Calories from Fat 5
	%Daily Value*
Total Fat 0.5g	1 %
Saturated Fat 0g	0 %
Trans Fat 0g	
Cholesterol 0mg	0 %
Sodium 0mg	0 %
Total Carbohydrate 28g	9 %
Dietary Fiber 3g	11 %
Sugars 18g	
Protein 1g	
Vitamin A 0% • Vitamin C 20%	
Calcium 0% • Iron 2%	

* Percent Daily Values are based on a 2,000 calorie diet.

LOW=5% or less HIGH=20% or more

1. Circle the grams of fiber on each label.
2. Which fiber-rich food will most likely help with digestion?

   ____

3. Which fiber-rich food helps with blood sugar and cholesterol? ______________________
4. What is one other nutrition fact you learned from reading the labels? ______________________

   ____

Name

What Is Cholesterol?

Our livers make cholesterol for our bodies. *Cholesterol* is a type of fat found in our blood and nerves. It is produced by the liver from some foods too, including meat, fish, eggs, butter, cheese, and milk. Some fats in foods raise cholesterol levels in your blood. Sometimes these fats raise the level too much. These types of fats are saturated fats and trans fats. There are also two types of cholesterol—LDL and HDL:

LDL carries cholesterol away from the liver and into the body. We say LDL is the "bad cholesterol" because it can stick to blood vessels. This can cause heart disease or a stroke in the brain.

HDL is the other type of cholesterol. HDL carries cholesterol back to the liver. The liver then breaks down the "bad" cholesterol. Exercise helps your body use good cholesterol. Some cholesterol can help us digest our food. Keeping a healthy weight can also help improve levels of HDL in your blood.

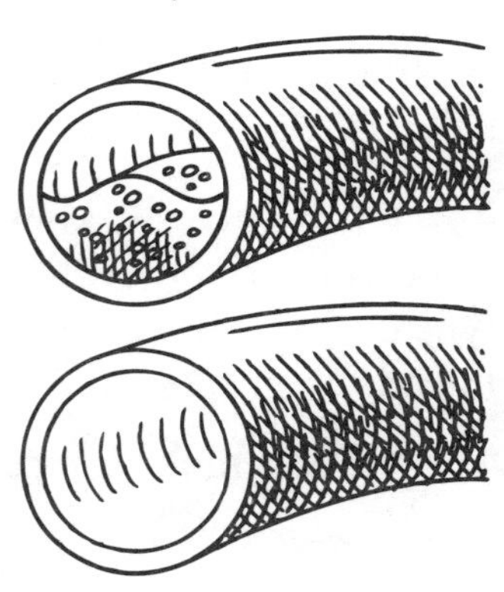

- Low cholesterol foods are often low in fat. These are healthy foods such as fruits, vegetables, and whole grains. These foods are good for most people.
- What does it mean when someone has "high cholesterol"? It means their bodies make too much cholesterol. Too much cholesterol can stick to the inside of the blood vessels and cause heart disease. This makes it hard for blood to flow to all parts of the body. The heart has to work harder. Exercise and eating lower cholesterol foods like fruits, vegetables, and whole grains can help. Avoiding foods with high fat content helps, too.

1. Write facts you have learned about good and bad cholesterol on the chart below.

"Good" Cholesterol HDL	
"Bad" Cholesterol LDL	

2. What is one way you can help your heart stay healthy? ______________________________

____

____

Challenge: Read food nutrition labels and compare the cholesterol in each. Find three foods that are low in cholesterol. List the cholesterol per serving underneath each food.

________________ ________________ ________________

________________% ________________% ________________%

Name

Sodium in Foods

Many foods have sodium in them. *Sodium* is the chemical name for salt. Your body needs salt in small amounts to keep the body fluids in balance. Salt also helps our nerves, our muscles, and our heart work the way they should. However, too much salt can be unhealthy. People who eat too much salt can have a greater risk for heart disease.

Every body is different, so how do you know how much salt your body needs? There is a range to consider, as well as personal health needs, height, weight, and activity level. Here is the suggested range:

4–8 year-olds ➜ 1,200–1,900 mg per day
9–13 year-olds ➜ 1,500–2,200 mg per day
14–18 year-olds ➜ 1,500–2,300 mg per day

These numbers can be helpful when looking at nutrition labels. It's very easy to get more sodium than we need in one day. Think about it—a baked potato (by itself) has only 15 mg of sodium, but an order of french fries has 135 mg of sodium. If you super-size it, the amount of sodium in the french fries increases to 350 mg. The more processed a food is, the more likely the amount of sodium is higher.

Directions: Collect nutrition labels from three foods. Look at the labels and find how much sodium is in a serving of each food. Write how much sodium is in each of the three foods you researched.

Food 1 ______________________ **Amount of Sodium** ____________________ **mg**

Food 2 ______________________ **Amount of Sodium** ____________________ **mg**

Food 3 ______________________ **Amount of Sodium** ____________________ **mg**

1. Add your three sodium totals.

Food 1 ______________________

Food 2 ______________________

Food 3 ______________________

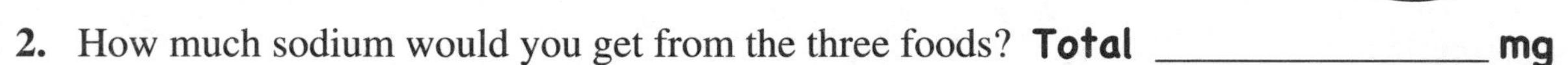

2. How much sodium would you get from the three foods? **Total** ______________ **mg**

3. Did you go over 1,500 mg? **Yes** _______ **No** _______

There are ways to lower your sodium intake if you think you are getting too much.

- Choose foods that are lower in sodium.
- Don't add extra salt to foods.
- Look on packaging for foods that are low in salt or sodium-free.
- Keep serving sizes in mind when you enjoy salted foods, and don't overdo it.

4. What could you do to lower the amount of salt in your diet? ______________________

____

____

Name

Add More Fruits and Vegetables!

For meals, half your plate should have fruits and vegetables on it. Having pieces of fruit or cut up vegetables for snacks is one way to add to the amount of fruits and vegetables you eat each day. Here are some other ways to add more of those healthy foods to your meals:

- Add veggies to spaghetti sauce. Try tomatoes, mushrooms, and olives. Get creative!
- Add vegetables to bean and meat chili.
- Stir vegetables into scrambled eggs.
- Mix fruits and veggies to make salads. Here are two recipe ideas:
  —Try sliced pears, sliced cabbage, grated carrots, and dried cranberries with orange juice drizzled on top.
  —Combine leafy green spinach, oranges, dried cranberries, and nuts, and toss.
- There is more to pizza than cheese! Add different veggies for a new taste treat. Try adding some green and red peppers, zucchini, or chopped fresh spinach.
- Create a vegetable skewer with a variety of chopped veggies and cherry tomatoes.

Directions: Use the ideas above and some of your own. Create recipes you would like to try. List your ingredients in the pizza, the salad bowl, and the smoothie outlines. Add fruits and vegetables to make them more healthful.

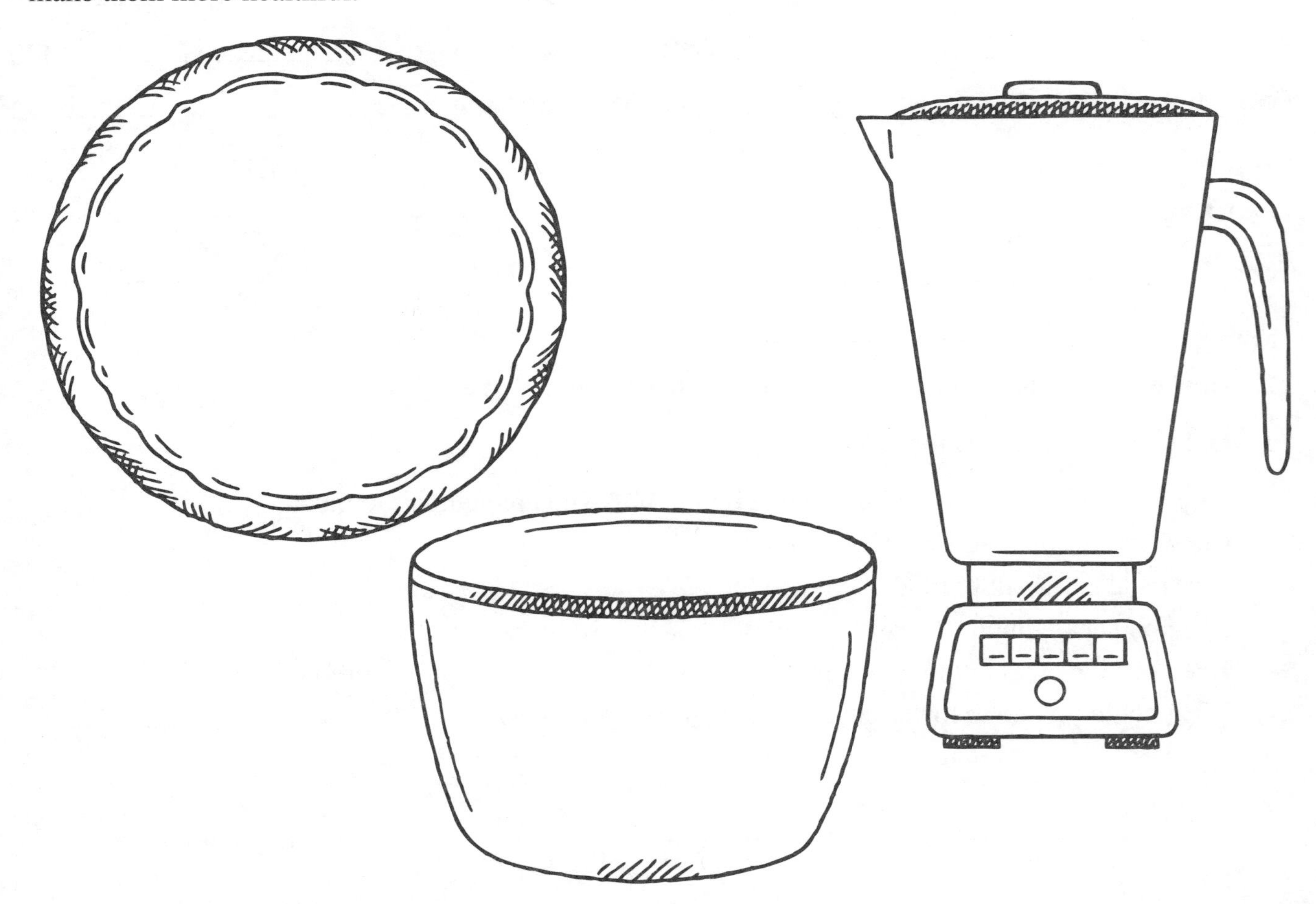

Name

My Plate—Revised!

By now you understand each of the food groups better. You may have tried new foods in each food group, too.

1. Diagram your favorite meal on the plate.

2. How many servings of each food group are in your favorite meal?

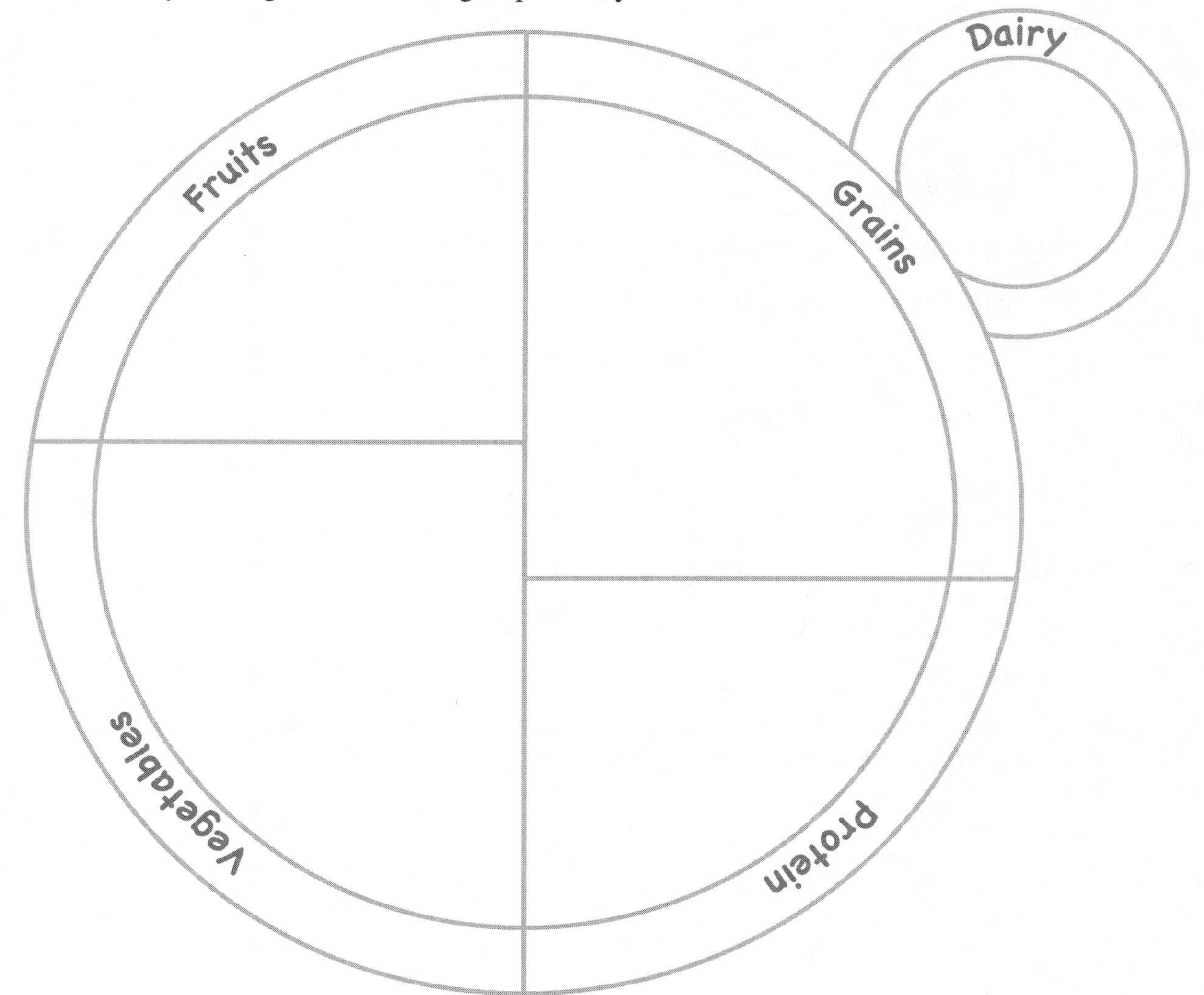

Do you want to adjust your favorite meal to make a healthier version? Think about switching foods rather than just adding. For instance, if your favorite meal is pepperoni and sausage pizza, perhaps you could switch and add your favorite vegetable to the pizza instead of one of the meats.

3. List some changes or substitutions you could make.

____

____

____

Name

Food Tips for Tip-Top Health

Are you in tip-top health? Read the tips and answer the questions that follow.

Food Tips

1. Learn to read nutrition labels. Remember to check the serving sizes and the amounts of healthy nutrients in each serving.
2. Enjoy your food without overeating. Portion your food on a plate according to the USDA recommended guidelines. Keep MyPlate in mind.
3. Throughout the day, try to eat foods from each group. Choose food products that are lower in sugar, fat, and sodium content.
4. Focus on fruits and vegetables by filling about half your plate with them.
5. Drink water instead of sugary soft drinks and juices.
6. Balance good eating habits with daily physical activity and get enough sleep.

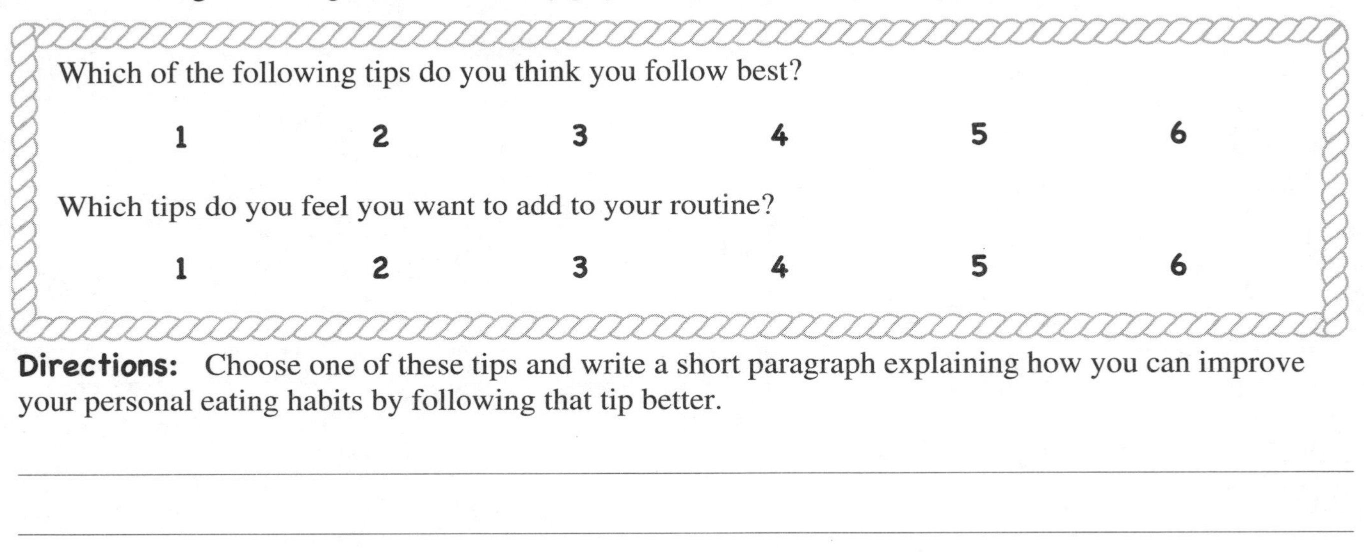

Which of the following tips do you think you follow best?

1 2 3 4 5 6

Which tips do you feel you want to add to your routine?

1 2 3 4 5 6

Directions: Choose one of these tips and write a short paragraph explaining how you can improve your personal eating habits by following that tip better.

____

____

____

____

____

____

Extension: Think about ways to practice healthy eating habits at your school. Research and compile a list of what schools across the country have done to promote healthy eating (e.g., healthy choices for hot lunch, or growing vegetables in a school garden).

Choose an idea you think should be implemented in your school. Write about how or why these changes could be made and give evidence. Use one of the blank pages in your journal.

Name

Food Safety

One way to make sure we benefit from eating healthy food is to follow food safety guidelines when preparing our food. There are several things we can do to make sure our food is safe and healthy to eat. Following food safety tips will help prevent food-borne illnesses.

- Begin by washing your hands with hot, soapy water before you touch food. Wash the fruits and vegetables before cutting or preparing them. Then, wash the cutting board with a disinfectant after you use it. Wash your hands, too, after handling food. This prevents the spread of harmful bacteria.
- Keep hot foods hot and cold foods cold. Perishable food should be kept cold. If food warms up over 40°, bacteria starts to grow. Once food has been cooked, it should be kept hot, over 140°, so bacteria can't grow. If cooked food will not be eaten within an hour or two, it should be refrigerated. If you are not sure food is still safe to eat, throw it out.
- Raw meat, poultry, and eggs have bacteria. This is why we cook meat and eggs and do not eat them raw. Keep raw meats away from other foods and wash counters thoroughly after preparing meat.
- Cover your mouth and nose when you sneeze. Be careful to turn your head away from the food you are preparing or eating. Wash your hands after sneezing or blowing your nose. This prevents germs from getting on food that people will eat.

Directions: Do some research to help answer these questions.

1. What are bacteria? ____________________

   ____

2. Are all bacteria bad? ____________________

   Why or why not? ____________________

   ____

3. What does *perishable* mean? ____________________

   ____

4. Name two perishable foods. ____________ ____________

Name

Sleep Is Good for Us

Whether we like it or not, sleep is an important part of a healthy lifestyle. Getting the proper amount of sleep affects how we feel and how we act. It helps to have a regular routine when going to sleep, and it is best to have a quiet room. Studies show that 10 or 11 hours is an appropriate amount for students 7–12 years old.

Why do we need a good night's sleep?

- While we sleep, our brain processes information, remembering what we have learned and experienced.
- With the right amount of sleep, we are able to pay attention and make better decisions.
- With the proper amount of sleep, we are more aware, which helps us stay safe and avoid accidents.
- People who do not get enough sleep take longer to finish tasks and make more mistakes.
- Tired people tend to be cranky people. Sleep helps us get along well with others.
- Sleep helps our bodies heal and fight infections. People who do not get enough sleep tend to get sick more often.

Take the quiz below to see how much you now know about sleep. Write **T** for true or **F** for false on the line next to each statement.

________________ **1.** Sleep is essential to our health and growth.

________________ **2.** The amount of sleep we get each night affects our energy the next day.

________________ **3.** Our brains and bodies need sleep.

________________ **4.** Sleep does not affect our memory and ability to do well in school.

________________ **5.** Sleep helps us solve problems and get new ideas.

________________ **6.** When we get enough sleep, we may have trouble listening, making good choices, or getting along with others.

________________ **7.** Preteens should get between 10 and 11 hours of sleep each night.

________________ **8.** It doesn't matter if you have a routine you follow each night.

________________ **9.** It's okay to have the TV or computer on when you're trying to sleep.

________________ **10.** It's a good idea to keep the bedroom dark, quiet, and cool.

A Perfect Night's Sleep

Do you have healthy sleep habits? **YES** ___________ **NO** ___________

11. What is one thing you might add or change in your own nighttime routine to help you sleep better?

____

12. What is one thing you might do in your bedroom to promote a healthier sleep environment?

____

Name

Protect Your Lungs!

When people refer to *wellness*, they are talking about a way of life. Several factors play a role in being well, or healthy. One, of course, is not being sick. Wellness also means not having risk factors for disease. You can reduce your risk by practicing healthy habits.

Let's look at one example of wellness. Let us focus on your heart, lungs, and blood vessels, which supply your body with oxygen. When you are well, these organs can do their jobs, especially when you are active. Eating healthy foods is one way to keep our heart and blood vessels healthy, but what about our lungs? One way to keep our lungs healthy is by not being around too many air pollutants.

1. What are pollutants?____

   ____

2. Name two air pollutants. ____________________ ____________________

We can't always control the air we breathe, but we can control some things related to our breathing. One smart, healthy choice we can make is to not smoke or use tobacco. Smoking is one of the most harmful things we can do to our bodies. But it is something we can choose not to do to remain healthy and live a longer, fuller life.

Smoking leads to more colds and coughs. The chemicals in cigarettes can lead to other diseases, too, including cancer. People who smoke have a harder time keeping up with others in physical activities, such as sports. Your lungs have a harder time moving oxygen through your body. This can make people who smoke more tired and grouchy.

3. List three reasons why smoking is not good for *your* health.

   - ____
   - ____
   - ____

4. What is second-hand smoke? ____

   ____

5. How can you avoid it? ____

   ____

Challenge: Work in groups to create posters or skits showing the benefits of living "tobacco-free." Be positive. What are the activities you can do, or do better, if you do not smoke? List reasons that you can give when someone tries to get you to smoke (e.g., "No thanks, I need to be able to run fast and for a long time to play basketball.")

Name

Pathway to Health

There are things we can do to stay healthy. We know we should eat healthy meals and exercise every day, but germs are everywhere! Test your knowledge of disease prevention by matching each healthy behavior to a way it helps promote good health. Think about how each behavior helps us avoid germs or helps our bodies in specific ways.

Directions: Write the letter for each explanation on the line in front of the statement.

Health Statements

_____________ **1.** Sneeze or cough into your sleeve.

_____________ **2.** Brush your teeth after meals.

_____________ **3.** Do not share drinks or eating utensils with friends.

_____________ **4.** Drink plenty of water.

_____________ **5.** Follow established safety rules and procedures.

_____________ **6.** Throw away used tissues.

_____________ **7.** Get enough sleep.

_____________ **8.** Practice good personal hygiene.

_____________ **9.** Ask a nurse or other trusted grownup if you have questions about health.

_____________ **10.** Wash your hands often.

Health Explanations

N—to make informed decisions about personal health, illnesses, and disease prevention
A—to prevent the spread of germs between friends
E—to keep teeth and gums healthy, and free of bacteria that causes disease
T—to prevent injuries and keep you safe
H—to protect other people from exposure to germs and bacteria
L—to help body organs and systems function properly
H—to protect other people from exposure to germs and bacteria
I—taking care of your body (e.g., bathing, washing hair, brushing teeth) helps maintain health
W—to keep your body rested, to build a strong immune system, and to fight disease
S—to prevent skin diseases and the spread of germs

Use the answers above to solve the puzzle. Place the letter for each answer (1–10) in the circle above its number. What does it say?

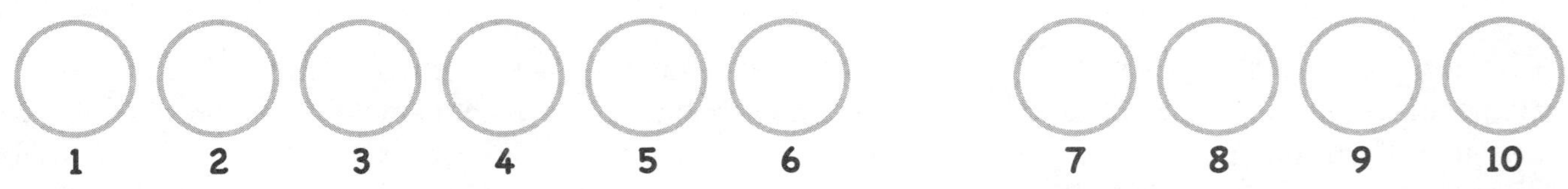

Challenge: Write a quiz question for a classmate to help him or her check his or her knowledge about disease prevention. Use the back of this page. Combine questions to create a class quiz.

Name

Stranger Danger

You may have had occasion to be by yourself or with friends without a grown up around. In any situation, even with trusted adults, it's important to be aware of your surroundings to stay safe.

Directions: Discuss the following questions in small groups. Take notes. Think about things you have heard or learned in school, at home, or in the community. Then, share your thoughts.

1. What might alert you that a person or situation is not safe? ______________________

   ____

2. What can you do if you sense you are in a potentially dangerous situation? ______________________

   ____

3. What things should you tell an adult before you go out alone?______________________

   ____

4. What guidelines do you have when you are home alone?______________________

   ____

5. What guidelines do you have for staying safe when using a computer?______________________

   ____

   ____

Challenge: Think of situations in which you might practice these safety tips.

1. Role play with your partner or a small group.
2. Present your skit to the rest of the group if time allows.

Sample dialogue:

Hey Mom, may I go to Ian's house?

Who will be there?

Jason is going to meet me at the corner and we're going to walk over together. Ian's mom will get home from work at 4:30.

When will you be home?

I'll be home by 6:00.

All right, call me if anything changes.

Okay. Bye, Mom!

Extension: What is the **NO-GO-TELL** strategy? Do some research to find out and write an explanation on a blank journal page.

Name

Healthy Lifestyles

There are many choices we can make to stay healthy. Talk with classmates to learn about different things people do to practice wellness.

Find classmates who have done each of the things listed on the chart. Have that person write their name and other information in the correct square. Try to have a different person write in each square.

______________ has made the choice to not smoke.	______________ ate a healthy breakfast. He or she had ______________.	______________ knows how to use the NO-GO-TELL strategy to stay safe.
______________ can name at least one food safety tip.	______________ had fruits and vegetables on half of his or her plate yesterday.	______________ has tried an alternate dairy or meat food. It was ______________.
______________'s favorite nut or seed is ______________.	______________ knows how many grain servings to have each day. ☐	______________ has tried a different kind of cheese other than cheddar or jack. It was ______________.
______________'s favorite cooked vegetable is ______________.	______________ likes fruit salad made with ______________ and ______________.	______________ got 10 hours of sleep last night.

Name

Staying Fit

Each day, we have a list of things we want to do and things we need to do. We go to school, do homework, do chores around the house, get together with friends, and spend time with our families. It's not always easy to find time for exercise. What are some ways people stay fit? Playing sports is a good way to get regular exercise. You and your friends may belong to a sports team. But not everyone plays a team or individual sport.

Here are some ways to work fitness into your everyday life:

- Stretch when you have a few minutes between assignments in class.
- Challenge yourself to work a little faster, reach a bit higher, or bend a little farther when doing chores at home.
- Ask a family member to park a little farther away from the store so you can walk together through the parking lot.
- Offer to take a younger sibling on a walk or bike ride around the neighborhood. You can get some exercise and help out family members at the same time. Better yet, see if you can get one of your parents to go with you. They need exercise, too!
- Ask your friend to walk with you or do something else that's active while you talk during lunch or breaks at school.

List three more ways to add a little more exercise to your day.

- ____

  ____
- ____

  ____
- ____

  ____

Challenge: Think about exercise-related activities that could be incorporated into the school day. It can be something as simple as lifting a book overhead 20 times or bending and stretching between classes. Encourage each other to be creative and think of realistic things.

Option 1: Work with a group to create a presentation for other classes to encourage people to add a little more exercise to their day and stay fit while at school. Each person in the group can make a drawing on a piece of plain white paper or a small poster. Put several of these together for the presentation or use presentation software on a computer.

Option 2: Make a set of *Exercise Reminders* posters that can be displayed around school to encourage fitness.

Name

Interval Training

A large part of being fit is our ability to be active. When we are healthy, our heart and lungs carry oxygen efficiently to all parts of our bodies. This, along with eating healthy foods, gives us energy to do the things we need and want to do.

People exercise to maintain physical fitness. There are many different ways to exercise. Often people **warm up** before they exercise. This means they do some types of movements at a less intense level than the actual activity. For example, before playing soccer, you might jog around the field once or twice or toss or kick the ball around a bit.

We can improve our fitness by doing different kinds of exercises. Sometimes people combine more than one activity into one exercise session. This is called **interval training**. It means you trade times of intense activity with lighter activity. For example, you might kick the ball around the track once, then run around the track once, and then kick the ball the third time.

Class Activity

1. Try a short interval activity. Alternate marching in place, a lighter exercise, and jogging in place, a more intense exercise. Switch activities every one or two minutes for a total of six minutes.

2. Brainstorm four more interval activities that can be done in the classroom. Do one each day for a week.

Interval Activity 1: March in place and then jog in place. Repeat.

Interval Activity 2: ______________________________

____

Interval Activity 3: ______________________________

____

Interval Activity 4: ______________________________

____

Interval Activity 5: ______________________________

____

Name

You Are a Fitness Machine!

The concept of fitness, or "getting in shape," may bring to mind an image of a gym. Many gyms have fitness machines to help people do a variety of exercises. Fitness machines use mechanical energy supplied by the person using the machine. People use these machines to build endurance and muscle. For example, many people use treadmills to walk or run for extended periods of time. Since the treadmill is stationary and inside, it doesn't matter what the road conditions or the weather is like!

Think about fitness machines you have used or seen in pictures or in a gym. They involve lifting, pushing, pulling, walking, running, or riding. What activities do you do each day that use similar movements? Write your ideas on the chart.

Lift	
Push	
Pull	
Walk	
Run	
Ride	

Challenge: Think of a way your body is like a machine. Explain.

____

____

____

____

____

____

____

Name

Fitness Survey

One way to get ideas for exercise and fitness activities is to find out what other students like to do. Do they walk everyday? Dance? Play on a team? Ride a bike or skateboard?

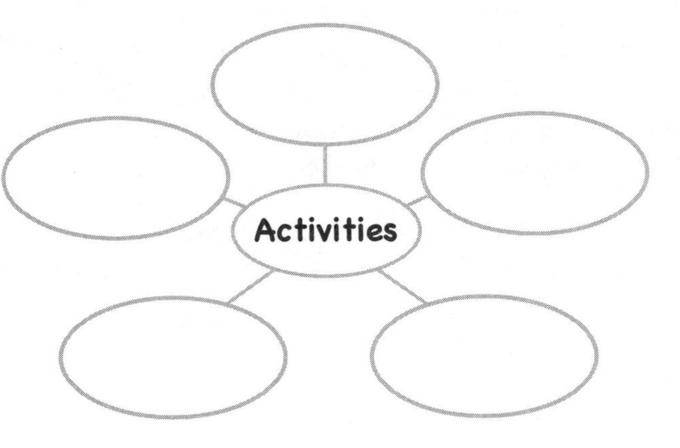

1. On a separate piece of paper, draw a web with your own activities.
2. Form small groups and brainstorm things you have done this week to stay active.
3. Combine the information to make a group "Fitness Survey" chart like the one below. Use tally marks to represent each person in each group.
4. Post all the groups' findings in a common area and review the data.
5. Note which activities were common, and which ones were more unusual.
6. Is there an activity the whole class can do? ______________________________

Fitness Survey				
Activity	**Group 1**	**Group 2**	**Group 3**	**Group 4**

Extension: Create a new class chart or grid to show the exercises done the following week. Keep listing new activities and add tally marks, stickers, or other markers each time the activity is done. Remember to include things like walking or riding your bike to school and P.E. or recess.

Compare the activities for the two weeks and discuss your results.

Name

Case for Fitness

Many elementary and middle schools have a physical education program. Students have P.E. one or more days a week. One elementary school has a unique fitness program. One day a week, fifth-graders play the role of "youth trainers." First, they take a fitness test. They learn about the test so they understand it before helping other students work their way through it. The youth trainers record peers' scores in fitness tasks to improve endurance and muscle strength. They take notes when other students participate in aerobic exercises.

The youth trainers lead activities to help their classmates improve in specific fitness areas. The other students play the role of "clients." The trainers work with teachers to set up fitness stations. At each station, one or more trainers explain to the clients (students) the fitness focus at that station. Trainers guide their clients through the activities at each station. Students rotate through the roles so that everyone has the opportunity to be a client with a fitness trainer and to train others.

At the end of the term, all students take the fitness test again. Students compare their fitness scores and reflect on the success of the training. Trainers and clients may make suggestions for improvement for the next term. The school also has a running club. The club meets two mornings a week before school. Students run around a marked track. Parents or other family members may also run. Members of the club receive a running stick every time they complete a lap. One hundred sticks equals 10 miles. When a student has completed 10 miles, he or she receives a "foot" token. Tokens are also awarded for marathons (26 miles) and super marathons (100 miles).

Now that you've read about how one school emphasizes fitness, think about your school.

1. What is one thing your school does to emphasize fitness? ______________________________

   ____

2. What might you or your class do to encourage people to make fitness part of their lives?________

   ____

Challenge

1. Divide into four or five groups. Each group will devise a fitness station and learn more about the proper way to do each task or action required. For instance, when stretching, you should move slowly and try not to bounce. If doing a runner's lunge, your knee should not move forward past your ankle.

2. Set up the stations with personal "recording sheets" for each participant. Have each person record his or her "starting ability" and then keep his or her sheet for recording new information each time.

3. Set a goal to practice one task or skill daily for a week and record the information. At the end of the week, see if the daily practice has led to improvement.

4. Add new stations as time allows. Consider having students take turns being "trainers," too.

Name

Sports

Playing sports helps us become fit in more than one way. Our heart and lungs need to be healthy to give us oxygen so we can keep moving. We use different muscles to run, jump, throw, or catch. These things are part of health-related fitness. We also use specific skills such as being able to change directions quickly. We need good balance to jump or catch a ball. Speed and power can help us do well in our chosen sport. Many of these things we develop through practice, but it also takes a bit of knowledge about the sport.

Directions: Think about a sport you know how to play or one you would like to learn. Do some research, if needed, to learn more about which skills are needed to play that sport.

1. Answer the following questions:

   Is it a team sport or an individual sport? ______________________________

   Which muscles do you use? ______________________________

   How does this sport help build endurance? ______________________________

   Which skills will you develop playing this sport? (agility, balance, speed, reaction time, etc.)

   ____

2. Draw a diagram to help you explain your sport to a classmate.

Sport: ______________________________

Name

Think Like an Athlete

We all have different abilities, but we can practice to improve our overall fitness. How do athletes stay in shape to do well in their chosen sport? They practice their skills and care for their bodies by getting enough rest and eating well.

Read each principle and its example. Think about how you can put each principle into practice in your life. Even if you don't play a certain sport, there are things you do to exercise and stay fit.

Principle	Example	Apply
Train all year for the sport, not just in the season.	*Hayley plays basketball in the fall and winter. She rides a bike and exercises in the spring and summer, too.*	
Practice a variety of skills.	*Ivan plays goalie on the hockey team. He practices shooting the puck and does different kinds of drills.*	
Exercise all the parts of your body.	*David runs in track-and-field races. He does exercises that strengthen his arms and the main part of his body, his core (torso).*	
Do exercises and movements similar to those found in everyday life.	*Kaylee likes to hike with her family and friends. She stays in shape all year by climbing stairs when she can't hike. Hiking helps her climb stairs in her everyday life. Climbing stairs helps her stay in shape for days when she goes for a hike.*	
Make agility training part of your exercise. This includes balance and flexibility exercises, too. Think of things you can do to improve coordination and speed.	*Kenneth and his friends get together and play soccer in Pedro's large backyard. Sometimes they set up an obstacle course where they run quickly and turn to dodge cones before they play.*	

Name

Careers in the Health Industry

It's a good goal to make overall health and wellness part of your everyday life. Some people choose to make it their career. Read the following descriptions of some health-related professions.

Dietitian/Nutritionist

A dietitian is an expert on food and nutrition. He or she helps people make good food choices for health. This job requires patience. Sometimes, people don't want to make changes, but their doctors or parents say they should. It takes a lot of time to help someone plan healthy meals with foods they like to eat. Sometimes dieticians plan menus for a large group of people. They have to work with the people who prepare the food. Dietitians have college degrees and pass special tests.

Physical Therapist

Physical therapists work with people to help them move without pain. They check people's coordination. They test muscle strength and range of motion. Sometimes, people are recovering from injuries or illnesses. A physical therapist goes to school for many years to learn what they need to know to help people regain motor function.

Coach

Coaches help players understand skills and strategies to succeed in sports. They also teach values that can be used outside the sports arena, such as the reward for hard work, the benefits of teamwork, and good communication skills. A coach goes to school but also practices learning under someone who is already a coach.

Personal Trainer

Personal trainers work one-on-one with clients. They also work with small groups. They help people learn and apply fitness principles. A good trainer can plan an exercise program for someone based on his or her age, physical ability, and risk factors. A good plan helps avoid injury and allows the person to get the most benefit from their exercise. A trainer thinks about the type of exercise a client enjoys and what will work with that person's lifestyle. A personal trainer goes through a training program to become certified.

1. Brainstorm other health-related professions.______________________________

   ____

   ____

2. Draw a star by the health-related profession that most interests you. It can be one of those mentioned above or one you brainstormed.

Challenge: Research the career you chose. Find out what you would need to do to pursue that career. What would you need to learn? What types of classes would you need to take? Add this information to the "Healthcare Professional" page in your journal (page 90).

Name

Healthy Habits Review

1. Think about everything you have learned about healthy foods and healthy habits. Use your "Making Healthy Choices" journal page (page 89) for notes.

2. Read over your notes and circle or highlight key ideas. List them here.

____

____

____

3. Discuss your thoughts with a partner or team.

4. Choose one of the following activities to summarize your learning. Share your completed project with the class.

Report Cube

Write a healthy habit on each face of a cube. Create a game to play with your classmates using the cube.

Alternatively, write something about a food from each food group on each face of a cube.

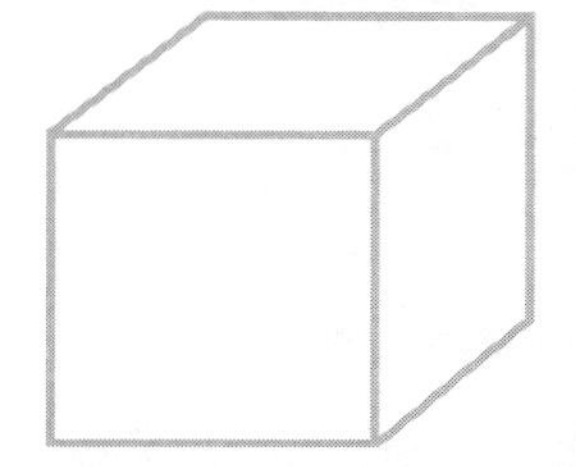

Postcard

Write a postcard about what you have learned. On one side of the card, draw a picture with a caption to summarize the content of the card. On the other side, write a message to a friend or family member about what you have learned. Include the person's address and mail the card to him or her.

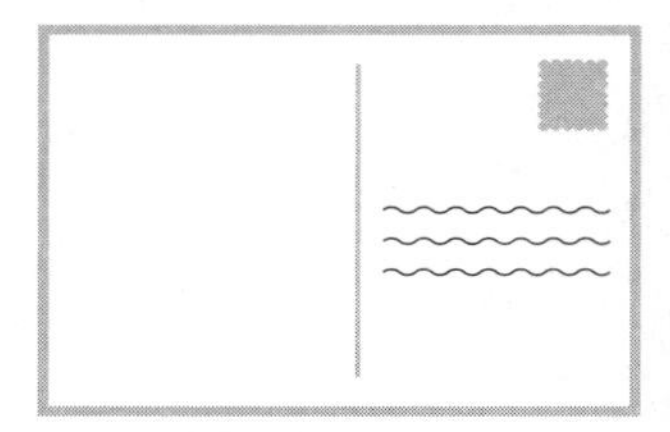

Brochure

Create a brochure about fitness. Think of one particular topic for your focus, such as healthy eating or fitness. Brainstorm your ideas for what you want to say. Consider including pictures, drawings, charts, graphs, or other graphics. Determine who will be most interested in your information (e.g., classmates, other people at school, or people in the community). Where might you distribute copies of your brochure? Use a word processing program or other publishing software to make a final copy. If possible, give copies of your brochure to your intended audience.

Food and Fitness JOURNAL

This journal belongs to:

Personal Health Goals

Directions: Write at least one personal health goal you would like to work towards each week. Check each week to see how you're doing at meeting your goal.

	Met	Not Yet
WEEK ____________________ My personal goal this week is to________________________________ ____		
WEEK ____________________ My personal goal this week is to________________________________ ____		
WEEK ____________________ My personal goal this week is to________________________________ ____		
WEEK ____________________ My personal goal this week is to________________________________ ____		
WEEK ____________________ My personal goal this week is to________________________________ ____		
WEEK ____________________ My personal goal this week is to________________________________ ____		
WEEK ____________________ My personal goal this week is to________________________________ ____		

New Healthy Foods

I have learned that it is important to eat foods from all five food groups. I have done research about one new food in each group. Here are my findings.

Fruit: ______________________________

Description: ______________________________

This food is grown in ______________________________

This food is good for me. It provides ______________________________

Vegetable: ______________________________

Description: ______________________________

This food is grown in ______________________________

This food is good for me. It provides ______________________________

Grain: ______________________________

Description: ______________________________

This food is grown in ______________________________

This food is good for me. It provides ______________________________

Dairy: ______________________________

Description: ______________________________

This food is grown or raised in ______________________________

This food is good for me. It provides ______________________________

Protein: ______________________________

Description: ______________________________

This food is grown or raised in ______________________________

This food is good for me. It provides ______________________________

My Garden Design

Garden Type: Hydroponic Container Garden In Ground

Garden Design:

Garden Plants:

______________________ ______________________

______________________ ______________________

______________________ ______________________

Other Materials:

______________________ ______________________

______________________ ______________________

______________________ ______________________

Where Do I Belong?

Directions: Choose from the food list below to create a healthy meal. Make sure you have foods from all the food groups.

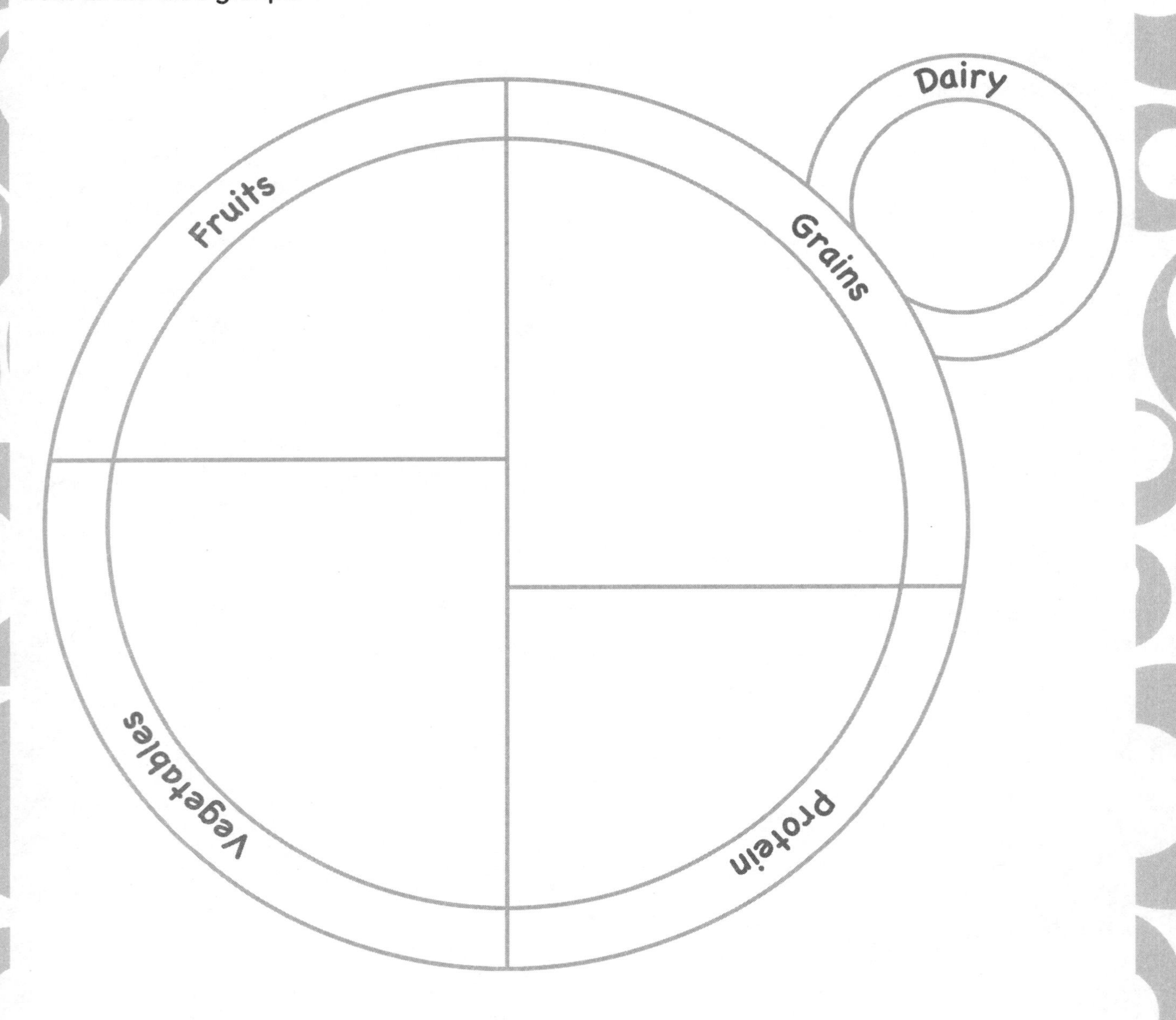

apples
asparagus
avocado
baked chips
beef
black beans
bread
broccoli
brown rice
carrots
cauliflower
celery
cereal
chicken
chickpeas
corn
cottage cheese
eggs
ham
lean pork
lemons
lettuce
milk
nuts
oatmeal
onions
pasta
peanut butter
pineapple
potatoes
pretzels
prunes
salmon
strawberries
string cheese
tofu
tortillas
tuna fish
yogurt

Local Foods

Try Me!

Imagine you are an organic food and that you are USDA approved. Write a letter to your class, convincing them to try you out. Explain why you might be a healthier option. Discuss how organic growers try to protect the people and the planet.

Track Your Servings

Fruits $1\frac{1}{2}$ cups per day	
Vegetables 2 cups per day	
Grains 5 one-ounce servings per day	
Dairy 3 cups per day	
Protein 5 one-ounce servings per day	

Was it easy to eat foods from all the food groups? ____________________

____

Did you eat more of something than you usually do? ____________________

____

Which food group is your favorite and why? ____________________

____

Does understanding serving sizes help you choose what you will eat? ____________________

____

Write about your experience. ____________________

____

____

____

____

Calories

1. What is a calorie?

2. What is an empty calorie?

3. What does it mean to supersize a meal? Discuss the pros and cons.

4. Based on what you have read and what you know, how would you define a "sometimes" food? Compare it to a healthy food.

5. Name a "sometimes" food you like to eat. How could it be made a healthier food, or what might be substituted for it?

Making Healthy Choices

Choosing healthy foods is important to me because...

Getting exercise every day is important to me because...

Healthy habits are important. Two things that I do to be healthy are...

Healthcare Professional

If I decide to be a healthcare professional, I think I would like to be a...

Journal Entry

Answer Key

Page 9—What Makes a Healthy Food?
Answers will vary.

Page 10—Healthy Foods Come in Groups
Answers will vary.

Page 14—Think About Fruit

1. nerves; muscles
2. energy
3. blood cells
4. lungs

Page 15—Growing Fruit
Answers will vary.

Page 16—Stone Fruits

1. plum
2. cherries; boron
3. Where they are grown: peaches are grown in California, South Carolina, and Georgia; apricots are grown in California and Washington. China and Italy are the leading producers of peaches; Turkey and Iran are the leading producers of apricots. Apricots are more often sold as dried fruit.
4. They are mostly harvested in the summer; they are high in vitamins A amd C, fiber, and potassium; all are stone fruits.

Page 17—How Well Do You Know Melons?

1. C
2. F
3. E
4. B
5. A
6. D

Page 18—Dragon Fruit
Answers will vary.

Page 19—Bunches of Bananas

Type	Yellow	Red	Manzano
Appearance	yellow; 7" long	dark red peel	yellow; 4" long
Vitamins	C	C, B6	C
Nutrients	fiber, iron, potassium	fiber, iron, potassium	fiber, iron
Flavors	banana	raspberry	apple
How to Eat	fresh, in baking	only when ripe; fresh, in baking; cooked with meat	only when ripe: fresh, in baking, fried
Grown	Central and South America	India, Central and South America	Africa, Central and South America

Pages 20–21—Think About Vegetables
Answers will vary.

Page 22—Different Kinds of Vegetables
Answers will vary.

Page 23—Culinary Vegetable Crossword

Across

1. eggplant
4. pumpkin
5. tomato
7. cucumber
8. squash
9. olive

Down

2. peppers
3. avocado
6. okra

Page 24—Culinary Vegetable Crossword

1. According to scientists, a culinary vegetable is a fruit since it has seeds inside. Since it is often cooked or served as a vegetable, it is often thought of as one!
2. fruit vegetable
3. avocado or olive
4. olive or avocado
5. pumpkin
6. cucumber

Pages 25–26—Peppers

Name of Pepper	Mild or Spicy	Characteristics
green bell pepper	sweet	turns red as it ripens
sweet banana pepper	sweet	looks like a banana
sweet cherry pepper	slightly spicy	looks like a small red bell pepper
Cubanelle pepper	spicy sweet	long and thin, pale yellow-green, turns red when ripe; sold as a spice or to roast
pepperoncini	mild pepper	also called Tuscan pepper; often sold pickled
jalapeño	spicy	between 2,500 and 8,000 heat units
red Fresno chili	spicy	works well in salsa
green Fresno chili	milder	use fresh
serrano chili	spicy	hotter than jalapeños
Anaheim chili	spicy; mild to hot	green when fresh; red when dried
habañero chili	spicy	green, then ripens to orange or red; much hotter than jalapeños

Answers to questions 3–5 will vary.

Page 27—Vegetable Family Tree

Carrots—root
Celery—stem
Fennel—root (bulb), stem (stalks), leaves, even seeds
Parsnip—root (bulb)
Caraway—seeds
Coriander—seeds; **Cilantro**—leaves
Cumin—seeds
Dill—leaves, seeds
Parsley—leaves
Answers to questions 1–3 will vary.

Page 29—All Kinds of Squash

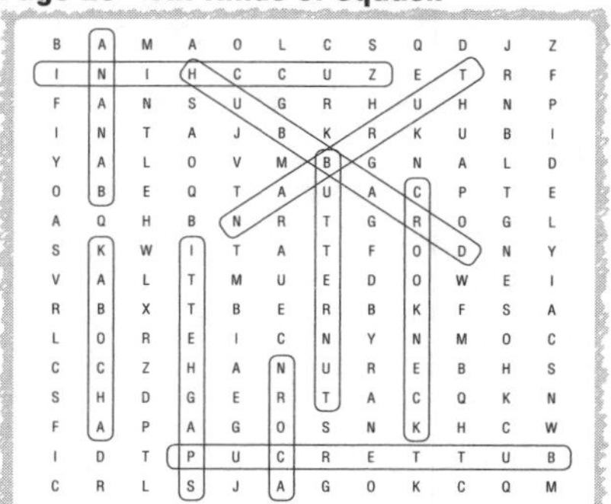

Page 30—Leafy Greens and Dark Green Vegetables

1. iceberg lettuce
2. 10
3. least nutritious
4. 11%
5. Answers will vary.

Page 31—Growing Vegetables in Small Places

Answers will vary.

Page 32—Think About Grains

Answers will vary.

Page 33—Corn

1. spoonbread
2. johnnycakes
3. hominy
4. grits
5. polenta
6. popcorn
7. cornmeal
8. hushpuppies

Page 34—Whole Grains

1. W
2. R
3. W
4. R
5. R
6. W
7. W
8. W
9. R
10. W
11. W

Page 35—What Does Gluten-Free Mean?

Answers will vary.

Page 36—Whole Grains–Spotlight on Sorghum

Sorghum is an important world-wide grain crop. Sorghum is a whole grain with an edible hull so we get all the nutrients. This ancient cereal grain is resistant to drought. For this reason, it is sometimes called the "camel of crops." It was grown thousands of years ago in Egypt and spread to all of Africa and then India. Today sorghum is grown in many countries around the world. In the United States, it is planted in the Midwest from South Dakota to Texas. The crop makes efficient use of sun and water. Most kernels are red, white, bronze, or brown, but they can be other colors.

Like corn, it can be used for food, animal feed, and fuel. In some countries, it is mostly used for food. Now, more people in the United States are using sorghum for food because it is gluten-free. People use sorghum in place of wheat flour in many traditional foods, such as pancakes, bread, muffins, and other baked goods. Countries around the world use sorghum in a variety of ways. In the Middle East, sorghum is used to make couscous and flatbread. People in Honduras use it to make tortillas. African countries make sorghum into porridge and flatbread.

Surprise your friends with these fun facts about sorghum! A variety of sorghum called broomcorn was introduced in the United States by Benjamin Franklin. What do you think it was used for? Making brooms! People in Africa dye some leathers red with red sorghum kernels. And finally, you can pop sorghum like popcorn.

Sorghum facts will vary.

Page 37—Think About Dairy Foods

Answers will vary.

Page 38—Types of Milk

1. buttermilk
2. pasteurization
3. reduced-fat milk
4. lactose
5. homogenization
6. whole milk
7. lactose-free milk
8. fat-free milk
9. flavored milk
10. fortified milk
11. low-fat milk

Page 39—Not All Milk Comes from Cows

Answers will vary.

Page 40—Say Cheese!

1. Cheddar cheese
2. Asiago
3. Gouda
4. Feta
5. Havarti
6. Monterey Jack
7. Provolone
8. Cottage cheese
9. Romano

Page 41—Fun with Dairy Facts

1. California and Wisconsin
2. Calcium is important for our health. Our nervous system, bones, heart, and muscles need calcium.
3. Milk provides many healthy nutrients including calcium, protein, vitamin D, and vitamin A.
4. Cheese is a good source of protein, calcium, and vitamins A, B2, and B12. Various cheeses provide other nutrients as well.
5. Yogurt is a source of good bacteria, protein, calcium, vitamin B2, B12, potassium, and magnesium.
6. Greek yogurt has a thicker consistency because more of the whey is removed. Greek yogurt has fewer carbohydrates, half the sodium, and a high protein content. Regular yogurt has three times the calcium of Greek yogurt. Both yogurts have similar calorie counts.
7. When milk is pasteurized it is heated. This process protects us from disease and helps the milk last longer.
8. Milk should last about a week past the "sell-by" date if it has been kept refrigerated. Always check, and if it smells funny, don't drink it. Lactose free milk lasts a month or more.
9. Answers will vary depending on age, gender, and activity level.
10. Whole milk has all of the fat left in, low fat milk has a small percentage of fat (1% or 2%) left in.
11. Ice cream and pudding are considered "sometimes" foods because they have added sugar.

Page 42—Think About Protein Foods

Answers will vary.

Page 43—Types of Protein

1. Possibilities will include:
   Complete Protein—meat, fish, poultry, cheese, eggs, yogurt, milk
   Incomplete Protein—legumes, grains, nuts, beans, seeds, peas, corn
2. Possible food combinations for complete protein:
   yogurt + seeds
   black bean + peanut salad
   spinach salad + sesame seeds
   cheese + pasta
   lentils + rice + peppers
   peanut butter + bread
   red beans + rice
   pinto beans + tortilla
3. Answers will vary.

Page 44—Do You Know Your Food Animals?

Bacon: pig
Hamburger: cow
Sausage: pig
Hot dog: pig; maybe cow (beef) or chicken
Steak: cow
Ribs: cow, pig
Wings: chicken
Taco: cow, chicken

1. bacon, pig
2. hamburger, cow
3. pig
4. cow

Page 45—All Kinds of Nuts

1. cashew
2. potassium, magnesium, and iron
3. Answers will vary.
4. Monitor discussions.

Page 46—Wild About Seeds

1. flax
2. poppy
3. caraway
4. sesame
5. sunflower
6. dill
7. pumpkin

Page 47–48—Fish and Shellfish Crossword

Across

2. salmon
3. perch
5. cod
7. scallops
8. trout
10. tilapia

Down

1. clams
2. shrimp
4. lobster
6. halibut
8. tuna
9. crab

Page 49—Legumes

1. Answers will vary. In general, legume snacks tend to be lower in calories and sugar content and have more protein.
2. Answers will vary.
3. Answers will vary.

Page 50—Local Foods

1. Answers will vary. Accept reasonable responses.
2. In general, the closer you live to where the food is grown, the fresher it will be.
3. One response might be that it would be interesting to try foods from different places.

Page 51—Organic Foods

1. It has not been grown or raised with chemicals or pesticides; livestock is fed organic foods.
2. Look for the USDA organic seal; read the label.
3. A preservative is something, often a chemical, that is added to food to keep it from spoiling.
4. People choose to eat organic foods because they are concerned about residue from pesticides, they do not want preservatives added to their food, and they are concerned about the environment.
5. Foods that have been grown or raised following specific guidelines can be labeled organic.
6. Organic foods conserve soil and water, reduce pollution, and make the best possible use of natural resources.

Challenge: In general, a natural food is one that does not contain artificial ingredients and/or is minimally processed.
Check student drawing of the USDA Organic seal.

Page 53—Look at the Label!

Answers based on label shown on page 52.

1. **Serving Size** 1 slice
   Servings per Container 6
   Calories per Serving 252
   Fat Calories 108
   Total Fat 12 g, 18%
   Saturated Fat 3 g, 15.%
   Cholesterol 30 mg, 10%
   Sodium 480 mg, 20%
   Total Carbohydrate 28 g, 9%
   Protein 8 g
   Sugars 5 g
   Vitamin A 4%
   Vitamin C 8%
   Calcium 20%
   Iron 4%
2. Answers will vary but, in general, the label provides information about the food product and gives us an idea of specific nutrients we may or may not be getting.

Page 54—What Counts as One Serving?

2 cups of pasta = **4** one-ounce equivalents of grain, or $\frac{4}{5}$ of your daily grain.

Page 55—What Counts as One Serving?

Answers will vary.

Page 56—Calories Review and discuss student journal page responses.

Page 57—Natural Sugar and Added Sugar

1. 2 servings per container
2. 19 g + 19 g = 38 g
3. Protein 3 g
4.

Food	Grams of Sugar per Serving	Teaspoons
barbeque sauce	13 g	3 teaspoons
chocolate bar	27 g	7 teaspoons
cola soda	27 g	6 $\frac{3}{4}$ teaspoons (average)
graham crackers	7 g	2 teaspoons
granola bars	8 g	2 teaspoons (average)
peanut butter	3 g	1 teaspoon
raisin bran cereal	16 g	4 teaspoons (average)
saltine crackers	0 g	0 teaspoons
spaghetti sauce	8 g (average)	2 teaspoons
yogurt	24 g	6 teaspoons

5. Answers will vary. Check the math.
6. The chocolate bar and cola soda or spaghetti sauce and granola bars have the same amounts of sugar.

Page 58—Natural Sugar and Added Sugar

1. 6 teaspoons equals 24 grams
2. no more than 24–28 grams of added sugar
3. cola soda
4. low-calorie cola
5. Milk has the most vitamins.
6. Milk. Milk provides vitamins A and C and calcium. Sodas do not. (Note: Milk also provides vitamin D.)

Challenge: Answers will vary.

Page 59—What is Fiber?

1. 8 g (kidney beans); 3 g (banana)
2. kidney beans
3. kidney beans
4. Check for reasonable answers.

Page 60—What Is Cholesterol?

1. **Good (HDL) Cholesterol:** carries cholesterol back to the liver; exercise helps your body use this type; can help us digest our food
   Bad (LDL) Cholesterol: carries cholesterol into the body; it can stick to blood vessels, this can cause heart disease or a stroke in the brain
2. Answers will vary, but should discuss exercise and healthy diet choices.

Challenge: Answers will vary.

Page 61—Sodium in Foods

Check for reasonable answers.

Page 62—Add More Fruits and Vegetables!

Check for reasonable recipes.

Page 63—My Plate—Revised!

Check for reasonable answers.

Page 64—Food Tips for Tip-Top Health

Check for reasonable answers.

Page 65—Food Safety

Check for reasonable answers.

1. Bacteria are microorganisms that are too small for the human eye to see. Some bacteria, or germs, can cause illness.
2. Some bacteria actually help us digest our foods and strengthen our immune systems. When talking about food safety, we are referring to the bacteria we try to protect ourselves from by handling raw and cooked foods correctly.
3. Perishable foods are those that will go bad if not stored properly. They can grow (bad) bacteria if left at room temperature and not put in the refrigerator or cooked in a timely manner.
4. Meat, poultry, eggs, and milk are some common perishable foods.

Page 66—Sleep Is Good for Us

1. T
2. T
3. T
4. F
5. T
6. F
7. T
8. F
9. F
10. T

11–12. Check for reasonable answers.

Page 67—Protect Your Lungs!

Check for reasonable answers.

1. Pollutants are things that make the air dirty and unhealthy.
2. smoke, air pollution from cars; possible air pollutants include carbon monoxide, lead, ozone, nitrates or soil particles, and sulfur oxides
3. leads to cancer; more colds and coughs; harder to do sports
4. Smoke from people smoking nearby
5. Answers will vary.

Page 68—Pathway to Health

H	E	A	L	T	H	W	I	N	S
1.	**2.**	**3.**	**4.**	**5.**	**6.**	**7.**	**8.**	**9.**	**10.**

Page 69—Stranger Danger

Answers will vary. Use the answers to discuss different safety measures.

Page 70—Healthy Lifestyles

Answers will vary.

Page 71—Staying Fit

Accept reasonable answers.

Page 72—Interval Training

Suggestions might include: side stepping/jumping jacks; marching/jogging; walking/skipping

Page 73—You are a Fitness Machine!

Accept reasonable answers.

Page 74—Fitness Survey

Accept reasonable answers.

Page 75—Case for Fitness

Accept reasonable answers.

Page 76—Sports

Accept reasonable answers.

Page 77—Think Like an Athlete

Accept reasonable answers.

Page 78—Careers in the Health Industry

Answers will vary.

Page 79—Healthy Habits Review

Check student projects for accuracy.